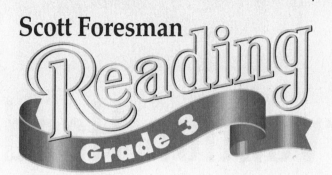

Scott Foresman
Reading
Grade 3

Intervention
Handbook

for Reading
Success

Scott
Foresman

Editorial Offices: Glenview, Illinois • Parsippany, New Jersey • New York, New York
Sales Offices: Parsippany, New Jersey • Duluth, Georgia • Glenview, Illinois • Carrollton, Texas • Ontario, California

© Scott Foresman 3

ISBN 0-328-02600-X

6 7 8 9 10 - V004 - 09 08 07 06 05 04

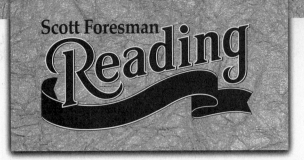

Scott Foresman
Reading

Intervention Handbook
for Reading Success

Contents
Section One

Section Two

About Section One of This Handbook

This part of the *Scott Foresman Reading Intervention Handbook* is a collection of strategies and blackline masters designed for those students who need additional support to successfully work through a lesson in the *Scott Foresman Reading* program. The strategies provide specific routines to use before, during, and after reading. The chart on pages 5 and 6 describes behavior manifested by students having reading difficulties and recommends an appropriate strategy routine.

When using the strategy routines, you will notice references to graphic organizers. For your convenience reproducible blackline graphic organizers can be found on pages 22–33. An explanation of the graphic organizers is on page 7. The strategy routines also list specific *Scott Foresman Reading* products you can use for intervention. A description of these products can be found on pages 8 and 9. One of the products listed is Leveled Readers A and B. A listing of comprehension skills and corresponding Leveled Readers, Grades 1–6, can be found on page 96.

How to Use Section One of This Handbook

The strategy routines are designed to be used with certain sections of the *Scott Foresman Reading* Teacher's Editions —Skill Lessons, Activate Prior Knowledge, Vocabulary, Guiding Comprehension, Reader Response, Phonics, Word Study, and Fluency.

Use these suggestions as a guide to approaching the strategy routines.

- Use the chart on pages 5 and 6 as needed. The *If … then* statements detail the kinds of reading problems students may have and direct you to a specific strategy routine to use.

- Read over the strategy routine before using it. Note any products or materials you may want to use with the teaching of the strategy routine.

- Proceed step by step through the strategy routine with students.

- Use the Apply and Assess to check students' understanding and application of the routine.

- Repeat the routine as necessary.

"Teachers should . . . demonstrate how to apply each strategy successfully—what it is, how it is carried out, and when and why it should be used. Instead of just talking about a strategy, teachers need to illustrate the processes they use by thinking aloud, or modeling mental processes, while they read."

Linda G. Fielding and P. David Pearson,
"Reading Comprehension: What Works"

> "... new information should be presented in a meaningful context and with substantial support from extra-linguistic cues such as visuals and demonstrations."
>
> Anna Chamot, Michael O'Malley, "The Cognitive Academic Language Learning Approach"

> "Making connections between images and definitions can help students remember word meanings."
>
> Camille Blachowicz, Peter Fisher, *Teaching Vocabulary in all Classrooms*

> "Children who are allowed to teach one another learn a valuable lesson in the process. They discover that people, even peers, can be good resources."
>
> Donald Graves, Virginia Stuart, *Write from the Start*

What Good Readers Do	Intervention		Strategy Routine
Good readers organize their thoughts as they read a selection.	**If . . .** students have trouble keeping track of the people or events in a story or article,	**then . . .** have them use graphic organizers to record their ideas.	**Use Graphic Organizers, p. 10**
Good readers set purposes for listening to a selection read aloud.	**If . . .** students have difficulty focusing their attention while listening,	**then . . .** help them set a purpose and record it before listening to a selection.	**Set a Purpose for Listening, p. 11**
Good readers use visual cues to understand and clarify vocabulary and concepts.	**If . . .** students do not have a clear understanding of how demonstrations and illustrations can help them,	**then . . .** demonstrate how these visual cues can be used to explain concepts.	**Use Visual Cues, p. 11**
Good readers make text meaningful by relating it to something in their own lives.	**If . . .** students have difficulty making a connection between their own lives and the text,	**then . . .** guide them to use an audio to build background.	**Use Audio to Build Background, p. 12**
Good readers use visual cues to build understanding.	**If . . .** students are uncertain how to use visual cues,	**then . . .** help them use pictures and demonstrations in order to relate to the text.	**Use Visual Cues, p. 12**
Good readers associate new vocabulary words with things from their personal experience.	**If . . .** students have difficulty calling upon prior knowledge to help them learn and remember unfamiliar words,	**then . . .** have them record words and pictures on a Vocabulary Frame.	**Use Graphic Organizers, p. 13**
Good readers use prior knowledge when they preview and predict.	**If . . .** students are uncertain about how to preview a selection and make predictions about it,	**then . . .** model how to use the text, the pictures, and your own knowledge to preview and predict.	**Preview and Predict, p. 14**
Good readers set specific reading goals.	**If . . .** students have difficulty setting a reading purpose,	**then . . .** help them focus their attention on setting a single purpose.	**Set a Purpose for Reading, p. 14**
Good readers enjoy and benefit from reading with others.	**If . . .** students are hesitant to read with others,	**then . . .** provide guidelines for reading with one or more classmates.	**Read with a Partner or Group, p. 15**
Good readers can follow along as a selection is read aloud.	**If . . .** students have difficulty following a selection as it is being read aloud,	**then . . .** guide them through an oral reading of the selection.	**Read Along with an Oral Presentation, p. 15**

FOCUS ON RESEARCH

"The important thing about self-corrections is that children initiate them because they see that something is wrong and call up their own resources for working on a possible solution."

Billie J. Askew, Irene C. Fountas, "Building an Early Reading Process: Active from the Start!"

FOCUS ON RESEARCH

"When the reading is phrased like spoken language and the responding is fluent, then there is a fair chance that the reader can read for meaning and check what he reads against his language knowledge."

Marie M. Clay, *Reading Recovery*

What Good Readers Do	Intervention		Strategy Routine
Good readers enhance their understanding and appreciation of text by relating it to their own personal experiences.	**If . . .** students have trouble connecting what they are reading with their own real-life experiences,	**then . . .** use a guiding comprehension question to model and explain how to relate text to personal experience.	**Relate Text to Personal Experience, p. 16**
Good readers know how to self-monitor and use fix-up strategies.	**If . . .** students are uncertain about when and how to help themselves when they are reading,	**then . . .** model how you monitor during reading by showing what you do when you don't understand something.	**Self-Monitor and Use Fix-Up Strategies, p. 17**
Good readers answer most questions about selections with confidence and success.	**If . . .** students have difficulty answering questions about selections,	**then . . .** present a routine for answering questions.	**Use a Routine to Answer Questions, p. 18**
Good readers know how to approach tests.	**If . . .** students have difficulty with test formats,	**then . . .** give them guidelines for taking tests.	**Use Test-taking Tips, p. 18**
Good readers can hear the sounds in words.	**If . . .** students have difficulty identifying the sounds that make up a word,	**then . . .** help them segment the word into its individual sounds and then blend those sounds to make the word.	**Use Blending and Segmenting, p. 19**
Good readers use decoding skills to figure out unfamiliar words.	**If . . .** students have trouble with letter-sound relationships,	**then . . .** demonstrate how word families can help students read and spell words.	**Use Word Families to Decode Text, p. 19**
Good readers understand how word parts combine and affect the meaning of a word.	**If . . .** students have difficulty recognizing and using word parts to figure out word meaning,	**then . . .** help students determine word meaning by identifying and defining the parts of the word.	**Use Word Parts to Understand Meaning, p. 20**
Good readers read fluently, decoding text automatically and focusing on meaning.	**If . . .** students read so slowly and laboriously, they cannot focus on meaning,	**then . . .** present a fluency routine they can practice using text that is familiar to them.	**Reread Familiar Text to Develop Fluency, p. 21**

About the Graphic Organizers

The following graphic organizers, found on pages 22–33, can be used with the strategy routines.

Vocabulary Frame is a creative way to get students to think about word meaning. Students activate prior knowledge by associating the word with something from personal experience. *Good for activating prior knowledge, predicting, and context clues.*

Story Prediction from Previewing calls upon students to use what they know as they preview the selection title and illustrations. Prediction activities motivate student interest, encourage readers to focus their attention, and give them a stake in the outcome of the story. *Good for predicting, activating prior knowledge, and drawing conclusions.*

Web 1 helps students highlight a central concept and connect it to related details. The web encourages students to generate ideas, recognize concept relationships, and organize information. *Good for main idea and supporting details and summarizing.*

Web 3 highlights a concept central to a selection or topic and allows students to relate and categorize details. Students who need help in connecting and organizing ideas will especially benefit from this organizer. *Good for main idea and supporting details and summarizing.*

K-W-L Chart helps students use what they know to generate interest in a selection. It encourages group members to share and discuss what they know, what they want to know, and what they learn about a topic. *Good for activating prior knowledge, setting purposes for reading, and summarizing.*

Plot/Story Sequence helps students recognize the sequence of events in a selection. Keeping track of the sequence of events is a simple way to give students a sense of story. Understanding sequence prepares students for more complex types of story structure. *Good for sequence, plot, recall and retell, text structure, and summarizing.*

Time Line helps students organize events from fiction and nonfiction in sequential order along a continuum. Not only do students see the events in order, but they are also exposed to the overall time frame in which the events occurred. *Good for sequence, summarizing, and text structure.*

Story Elements provides a framework for thinking that can help students write a summary of a story. It is particularly useful for students who need more guidance recognizing story structure and summarizing key events. *Good for character, setting, plot, theme, summarizing, sequence, and drawing conclusions.*

Cause and Effect helps students identify what happened and why it happened in both fiction and nonfiction. When students can see that there are causal relationships between events or ideas in text, they can make generalizations about other causal relationships in new texts and in life situations. *Good for cause and effect, summarizing, sequence, and text structure.*

Problem and Solution 1 helps students identify problems and solutions presented in fiction or nonfiction. It prompts students to recognize what is important in the story and how ideas or events are related to a problem. *Good for plot structure, summarizing, and text structure.*

T-Chart provides a visual framework to help students identify two items or concepts. Students can use the graphic organizer to chart ideas within a text, across texts, and between prior knowledge and new ideas. *Good for compare and contrast, main idea and supporting details, summarizing, and activating prior knowledge.*

Five-Column Chart provides a grid on which students can organize information for clearer understanding. It is a useful tool for exploring and classifying ideas, story elements, genres, or vocabulary features. *Good for compare and contrast, main idea and supporting details, summarizing, and activating prior knowledge.*

About *Scott Foresman Reading* Products

These Scott Foresman products are referenced within Section One of this handbook and are part of the *Scott Foresman Reading* program.

AstroWord is an interactive CD-ROM program that allows students to learn and reinforce word study, phonics, and vocabulary skills. Each activity follows the teach, practice, and apply instructional model. The setting for *AstroWord* is an intergalactic factory that supplies words to alien customers to help them solve word-related problems. Students listen, write, manipulate words, and play games.

Background Building Audio Cassette/CD helps students get ready to read the selection in the basal by building background and drawing upon their prior knowledge. Author interviews, radio broadcasts, historical recordings, and scene-setting sound effects encourage visualization and support concept development.

Comprehension Strategy Posters are part of the *Scott Foresman Reading Adding English* product. Each poster depicts one comprehension strategy using situations familiar to all students. The posters list clue words students need to discuss and use the strategy, suggestions for presenting the strategy, and leveled activities. Eleven Comprehension Strategy Posters accompany the *Adding English Guide: ESL Teacher's Guide*.

Daily Word Routines Flip Chart provides quick activities for students to practice phonics, word study, vocabulary, and language.

Grade 3 *Phonemic Awareness and Phonics Manipulatives Kit* helps students practice phonics and word-building through hands-on activities and multi-sensory games.

Grade 3 *Phonics Sourcebook* provides blackline masters of words and letter manipulatives and games from the *Phonemic Awareness and Phonics Manipulatives Kit*. If the kit is not accessible, the sourcebook can be used in its place.

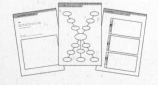

Graphic Organizer Transparencies help students build comprehension, learn how to organize information, and model higher-thinking skills. They may be used to model how students complete their own graphic organizer.

© Scott Foresman 3

Leveled Readers A and B are for those students needing a lower-level reading selection. They are written one to one and a half grades below grade level. For every main selection in the basal Student Edition, there is a corresponding Set A Leveled Reader (Easy) and a Set B Leveled Reader (Easy/Average). The books reinforce each lesson's target comprehension skill and provide practice with the selection vocabulary. See page 96 for an overview of *Scott Foresman Reading A* and *B Leveled Readers* in Grades 1–6. For your convenience, the Leveled Readers are listed according to the comprehension skills they cover.

Leveled Reader Resource Guide includes instructional plans and practice for each Leveled Reader. The guide provides strategies for guided reading, vocabulary development, and on-going assessment.

Scott Foresman Know Zone™ website helps students prepare for tests by providing test-preparation techniques, practice, and reinforcement. Log on to the Know Zone™ at www.kz.com or connect to it through the *Scott Foresman Reading Headquarters Website.*

Scott Foresman Reading Headquarters Website, at www.sfreading.com, offers Internet Workshops that extend the Student Edition selections by having students investigate a topic on the Internet, then write ideas, and share them with their class.

Selection Audio Cassette/CD includes recordings of all Student Edition selections in the basal. The selections are recorded to allow students, especially those working below level, to follow along as the selection is read aloud.

Ten Important Sentences is a booklet that provides the ten most important sentences for every main selection in the basal Student Edition. Each sentence in the booklet includes a key idea from the selection to help build the skills students need for comprehension. Blackline masters, strategies, and activities for using the sentences are included in the booklet.

TestWorks for Scott Foresman Reading is a CD-ROM that allows teachers to customize multiple-choice tests, free-response tests, and practice tests for students.

Strategy Routines for Skill Lessons

Use Graphic Organizers

About the Strategy

Mapping out a concept can help students understand what they read. Graphic organizers can help students improve reading comprehension skills as they move from mere memorization tasks to real learning experiences.

How to Use the Strategy

1. **Introduce** the idea of a graphic organizer to students. Explain that it will help them organize their thoughts as they work through a reading selection.

2. **Select** a graphic organizer appropriate for the skill lesson selection students are currently reading.

3. **Display** the graphic organizer as an overhead transparency or as a blackline master.

4. **Read** through the graphic organizer with students. Always partially complete the graphic organizer with them. This will help students focus and understand what they are doing and why.

Apply and Assess

Students can work independently, in pairs, or in small groups to complete the graphic organizer. Bring the group back together to discuss the information they recorded and how the organizer helped.

The following is a list of graphic organizers you can use with skill lessons. See page 7 for a description of each organizer and the skills it can support. Graphic organizers in blackline master form can be found on pages 22–33.

Story Prediction from
   Previewing, p. 23
Web 1, p. 24
Web 3, p. 25
K-W-L Chart, p. 26
Plot/Story Sequence, p. 27

Time Line, p. 28
Story Elements, p. 29
Cause and Effect, p. 30
Problem and Solution 1, p. 31
T-Chart, p. 32
Five-Column Chart, p. 33

If available, you may want to use the *Graphic Organizer Transparencies.*

Set a Purpose for Listening

About the Strategy

Setting a purpose for listening helps students focus attention while listening.

How to Use the Strategy

1. **Introduce** the skill lesson selection by going over the title, author, and any illustrations. Ask students what they would like to find out or set a purpose for students.

2. **Work** with students to write a statement or question that reflects the purpose. For example: Listen to find what Meg likes and dislikes about baseball.

3. **Discuss** the selection after students have listened to it. Refer back to the sentence to keep students focused. Use a graphic organizer, such as the T-Chart, to keep track of the discussion.

Apply and Assess

Students can write a brief paragraph or make an illustration to demonstrate an understanding of the purpose they listened for.

If available, you may want students to listen to the skill selection read aloud on the *Selection Audio.*

Selection Audio

Use Visual Cues

About the Strategy

Visual cues such as pictures or demonstrations may help students understand vocabulary and concepts, such as cause-effect relationships.

How to Use the Strategy

1. **Show** a picture or demonstrate the skill with props. For example, for the skill of cause and effect, show a picture of a shattered glass. (Always choose pictures that will be familiar to your students.)

2. **Describe** or have students describe the picture.

3. **Ask** students literal and inferential questions about what they see. Phrase questions so that students focus on the skill. For the picture of the shattered glass ask students what they see. Ask what might be a reason (cause) that the glass shattered (effect).

4. **Record** students' responses on the Cause and Effect or T-Chart graphic organizer.

Cause	Effect

Apply and Assess

Present a new visual cue for the skill or for a different skill. Students can work in pairs or small groups to complete a graphic organizer for the skill. Have students share completed organizers with the group, telling what visual cues helped them.

If available, you may want to use *Comprehension Strategy Posters* from *Adding English* for teaching a comprehension skill using visual cues.

Strategy Routines for Activate Prior Knowledge

Use Audio to Build Background

About the Strategy

To hear a cow mooing or the sound of a train whistle can help students relate a selection to their own lives. Building background through audio can help students make reading the text more meaningful.

How to Use the Strategy

1. **Introduce** the contents of the CD/tape. If students will be listening to a speaker, sound effects, or a song, discuss it first. Guide students in setting a purpose for listening. Have students write it down.

2. **Discuss** the contents of the CD/tape after students have listened.

3. **Record** on the board or graphic organizer students' thoughts.

4. **Replay** the tape as needed for further discussion or for clarification.

Apply and Assess

Students can work together or individually to complete a graphic organizer about the recording. Bring the group back together to discuss what they wrote and what they learned from the audio.

If available, you may want students to listen to the *Background-Building Audio.*

Background-Building Audio

Use Visual Cues

About the Strategy

Visual representations engage students before they read. Visual cues such as pictures, demonstrations, or dramatizations help build understanding.

How to Use the Strategy

1. **Show** a picture or do a demonstration of something related to the selection students will be reading. For example, if the story is about baseball, use a ball and a bat to introduce the selection.

2. **Help** students relate the visual cue to something in their own lives.

3. **Use** graphic organizers, such as the T-Chart or Five-Column Chart, to capture students' ideas and thoughts related to the selection.

Apply and Assess

Using the graphic organizer, students can work individually or in pairs to write a list of items that they think will relate to the selection. Have students tell what the item is and how it relates.

If you have access to the *Scott Foresman Reading Headquarters Website,* you may want to visit the Internet Workshop section at www.sfreading.com to expand upon ideas in the selections students will be reading.

© Scott Foresman 3

Strategy Routine for Vocabulary

Use Graphic Organizers

About the Strategy

Using graphic organizers, such as a Vocabulary Frame, can help students think about word meaning by associating words with something from personal experiences. Calling upon prior knowledge can help students predict, learn, and retain the meanings of unfamiliar words.

How to Use the Strategy

1 Limit the number of new words students need to know. Share the words and discuss their meanings with students.

2 Work through the Vocabulary Frame graphic organizer on page 22 with students. Students can have their own copy of the organizer, writing along with you. Write a vocabulary word, such as *instruments,* in the word box. Ask students to suggest a picture or symbol they think might help them remember the meaning of the word. Then draw the image in the association box. Students should put this same information on their organizers.

3 Ask a volunteer to suggest a definition for the word and then give a sentence using it. Write the definition and sentence on the organizer. Students should write this definition and sentence on their copies.

4 Verify the definition by having students use a dictionary or glossary to find the word. Write this definition on the appropriate lines and have students do the same.

5 Have students provide a second example sentence based on the verified definition and write this sentence on their organizers.

6 Repeat as necessary using other words.

Apply and Assess

Students can work individually or in pairs to complete Vocabulary Frames for other new words they are learning. Bring the group back together and have them share their organizers for each of the words.

Other graphic organizers that can be used for vocabulary include the following: Web 1, p. 24; Web 3, p. 25; T-Chart, p. 32; Five-Column Chart, p. 33.

· ·

If available, you may want to use any or all of these products for more vocabulary practice: the *Graphic Organizer Transparencies* and the *Daily Word Routines Flip Chart.*

· ·

Strategy Routines for Reading Strategies

Preview and Predict

About the Strategy

By previewing a selection, students can draw upon what they already know to understand what they are about to read. Previewing helps students formulate predictions based on prior knowledge.

How to Use the Strategy

1. **Read** aloud or have a student read the title, author, and a paragraph or two. Have students look at any illustrations or photographs.

2. **Model** using the text and pictures to predict what a selection will be about. For example, for the story "Addie in Charge," say, "The head-note tells that Addie has been left in charge of the farm. I know that pioneer children know a lot about farming. The pictures show that Addie faces a fire. I predict that Addie will not save the farm but will save herself and her brother."

3. **Write** your prediction on the board. Have students work individually, in pairs, or small groups to write their predictions.

Apply and Assess

Bring the group back together to compare and explain their predictions.

If available, use *Leveled Readers A* or *B* for lower-leveled selections to preview and predict.

Set a Purpose for Reading

About the Strategy

Setting a purpose before reading helps students establish a clear focus and enables them to direct their attention to a specific reading goal.

How to Use the Strategy

1. **Preview** the selection by reading the title, author, introductory notes, if they exist, and/or a paragraph or two.

2. **Ask** students what they hope to find out when they read the selection. Write their responses on the board.

3. **Use** the list on the board to set a single purpose with students for reading. Discard all other responses.

4. **Begin** a graphic organizer such as a K-W-L chart with students to help them organize their thoughts.

K What I Know	W What I Want to Know	L What I Learned

Apply and Assess

As they read, students can work individually or in pairs to complete the graphic organizer. Bring the group together to discuss the organizer.

If available, use *Leveled Readers A* or *B* for lower-leveled selections to set a purpose for reading and the *Graphic Organizer Transparencies*.

Read with a Partner or Group

About the Strategy

As students read with a partner or group, they increase comprehension and confidence to read better as they interact and discuss what was read.

How to Use the Strategy

1 **Choose** for students a partner or small group to read the selection with. If pairing, pair a less fluent reader with a more fluent reader.

2 **Write** the following partner reading cues on a chart or the board.
  a. Decide who will read first.
  b. Decide where to stop and switch readers.
  c. Stop and discuss sections you don't understand.
  d. After reading, talk about what you have read.

3 **Monitor** the reading from a distance and check progress after students have finished.

Apply and Assess

Students can track their reading by using a graphic organizer such as Problem and Solution 1 or by taking notes and writing a brief summary. Let students share their notes with the group.

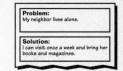

Problem:
My neighbor lives alone.

Solution:
I can visit once a week and bring her books and magazines.

If available, use *Leveled Readers A* or *B* for lower-level selections to read and the *Graphic Organizer Transparencies*.

Read Along with an Oral Presentation

About the Strategy

Hearing a selection read aloud can make the text come alive for students. When students read along as a selection is being read aloud, they often gain confidence to read it by themselves.

How to Use the Strategy

1 **Decide** who will read the selection aloud. Will you read it aloud, will an audio version be played, or will students take turns reading?

2 **Set** guidelines for readers to follow, such as stopping at certain points, reading with expression, or changing voices to suit the material.

3 **Have** students follow along as the selection is read aloud. You may want to stop at predetermined spots for clarification or questions.

4 **Work** with students to summarize the most important ideas.

Apply and Assess

Students can use a graphic organizer, such as Plot/Story Sequence, to summarize what they have learned as they listened to the story being read.

If available, you may want to use any or all of the following products: the *Selection Audio* for students to hear the selection read aloud, *Ten Important Sentences* to help students summarize, and the *Graphic Organizer Transparencies*.

Selection Audio

Strategy Routines for Guiding Comprehension

Relate Text to Personal Experience

About the Strategy

Relating text to students' life experiences helps students become more involved with what they read and increases their comprehension, appreciation, and motivation to read.

How to Use the Strategy

1 **Choose** one of the guiding comprehension questions in the *Scott Foresman Reading* Teacher's Edition. Write it on the board or use a graphic organizer such as Web 1 or Problem and Solution 1.

2 **Model** how you would answer the question. For example: *Question:* Why do you think Marianne touches the feather in her pocket as she says, "She'll be there. She'll want me." *Answer:* I think Marianne is hoping to find her real mother. I think Marianne is touching the feather for good luck. By touching the feather, it makes her feel calm and assured that her mother just might be there.

3 **Relate** your answer to a personal, real-life situation or make a cross-content connection. For example, you might say, "Sometimes when I watch my daughter play a basketball game, I cross my fingers when she takes a shot. I know that her talent and practice will help her make the shot, but I still cross my fingers for luck. I think Marianne is touching the feather for the same reason. What do you think?" Allow students time to offer their opinions.

4 **Guide** students through another question in a similar manner. Have students relate their answers to a personal, real-life situation.

Apply and Assess

Have students work in pairs or small groups to answer one or two of the guided reading questions about the selection. Questions can be written on the board or on a graphic organizer. The group can come back together and share their answers.

If available, you may want to use the *Leveled Readers A* or *B* for lower-level selections and the accompanying *Leveled Reader Resource Guide* which contains guiding comprehension questions.

Self-Monitor and Use Fix-Up Strategies

About the Strategy

Learning when, where, and how to self-monitor and use fix-up strategies can help students check their reading comprehension, enabling them to become independent, fluent readers.

How to Use the Strategy

1 Demonstrate what you do when you are reading and don't understand something. Explain that you stop reading and try to identify what is causing the confusion. For example, say: "I've read a few pages, and a lot has happened already. I understood everything until this last part—it doesn't make sense to me. I think I should stop reading and ask myself: What things have happened so far in this story? Did I miss something that's important? What should I do now?"

2 Model using an appropriate fix-up strategy. For example, for the strategy of reread and review, say: "I will read this page again. I am not sure why Laura was afraid of the badger. I will read the page again more slowly to see if there's something I missed."

3 Focus on only one fix-up strategy at a time, such as reread and review. Students should practice one fix-up strategy over a period of time until they are able to do the strategy themselves without prompting or help.

4 Use a graphic organizer so students can organize their thoughts. You may want to continue the graphic organizer students began in Activate Prior Knowledge or begin a new graphic organizer such as a K-W-L chart or a graphic organizer that better fits a particular skill such as sequence.

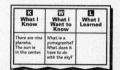

The following are some fix-up strategies you may want to use with students.

adjust reading rate	seek help from reference sources
read on	skim and scan
reread and review	use text features
seek help from others	write notes

Apply and Assess

Have students work in pairs to complete a graphic organizer together. Have them record the fix-up strategy they use on the organizer. Remind partners to stop reading when one of them doesn't understand something and to use the fix-up strategy. Bring the group back together after reading. Have pairs summarize what they have read and how the fix-up strategy helped them.

If available, you may want to use the *Graphic Organizer Transparencies*.

Strategy Routines for Reader Response

Use a Routine to Answer Questions

About the Strategy

When given a routine to answer questions about a selection, students can answer the questions with confidence and success.

How to Use the Strategy

 Discuss the following routine with students.
   a. *Read each question carefully.* This can help students decide what information is being asked for.
   b. *Put the question in your own words.* This can help students figure out what a question means or what information is needed.
   c. *Reread the text.* This can help clarify meaning or explain an answer.

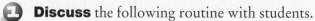 **Work** through a question with students using the routine and a Five-Column Chart graphic organizer.

Apply and Assess

Students can work in small groups to answer each remaining question using the Five-Column Chart graphic organizer. Groups can share and discuss their responses.

If available, you may want to use the *Graphic Organizer Transparencies.*

Use Test-taking Tips

About the Strategy

When students understand how to take a test, they perform better and become more confident in their answers.

How to Use the Strategy

 Write the following test-taking tips on a chart or the board.
   a. Read all the directions carefully before you begin.
   b. Read the entire question and all the choices before trying to answer multiple-choice questions.
   c. Look for key words that signal what is needed for the answer.
   d. Skim the selection to find related phrases or sentences that might contain the answer.
   e. Eliminate answer choices that are clearly incorrect in multiple-choice questions.

 Demonstrate each tip, using a test students have already taken.

Apply and Assess

Have students complete a practice test. Upon completion of the test, have them explain what test-taking tips they used and how the tips helped.

If available, you may want to log on to the *Know Zone*™ at <u>www.kz.com</u> or connect to it through the *Scott Foresman Reading Headquarters Website* at <u>www.sfreading.com</u> to do a practice test. You can customize tests for students using *TestWorks for Scott Foresman Reading.*

© Scott Foresman 3

Strategy Routines for Phonics

Use Blending and Segmenting

About the Strategy

Blending and segmenting is a crucial phonemic awareness skill students need to develop for decoding and syllabication. When they can hear the sounds in words, they can associate those sounds with letters.

**How to Use
the Strategy**

1. **Say** a vocabulary, spelling, or one-syllable word such as *tops* slowly. Have students repeat it. Ask how many sounds they hear. (4)

2. **Segment** the sounds in the word, saying each sound /t/ /o/ /p/ /s/. Have students say the sounds after you.

3. **Blend** the sounds together. Have students blend the sounds together to say the word: *tops.* Tell them to listen for all four sounds.

Apply and Assess

Present pictures of one-syllable words such as a cat and a coat. Working with one word at a time, say each sound in the word. Have students blend the sounds to say the word and point to the picture being named.

If available, you may want to use the Grade 3 *Phonics Sourcebook* or the Grade 3 *Phonemic Awareness and Phonics Manipulatives Kit* for visual or kinesthetic learners.

Use Word Families to Decode Text

About the Strategy

Using word families can help strengthen students' decoding skills as they recognize the relationship between words that sound the same.

**How to Use
the Strategy**

1. **Write** on the board and say a word that students know, such as *round*.

2. **Ask** students to name other words that rhyme with *round*. Write students' responses on the board.

3. **Circle** the similar part of each word, such as the *ound* in *round*. Help students recognize that only the initial letter or letters change, and if they can read and spell a word such as *round*, then they can read and spell other words with a similar sound.

4. **Repeat** as necessary with other words.

Apply and Assess

Have students work in pairs or teams to make word families from ending sounds, such as *ate, ight, ash,* and *oon*. Students can share their words.

If available, you may want to use the Grade 3 *Phonics Sourcebook* or the Grade 3 *Phonemic Awareness and Phonics Manipulatives Kit.*

Strategy Routine for Word Study

Use Word Parts to Understand Meaning

About the Strategy

Recognizing word parts and understanding how they combine and contribute to the meaning of a word, can help students determine the meanings of unfamiliar words.

How to Use the Strategy

1. **Write** on the board a sentence containing a compound word or a word with an affix or ending. Examples: *The children dislike that game. Where is the cookbook? The puppy is playful.* Have students read the sentence.

2. **Circle** the word you want students to focus on, for example, *dislike, cookbook,* or *playful.* Discuss its meaning.

3. **Write** the word again and underline the affix, ending, or two words that make up the compound word.

4. **Explain** or let volunteers explain the meaning of any word part and how it affects the meaning of the word. For example: When *dis-* is added to the word *like,* it makes the word mean the opposite. *Dislike* means "to not like."

5. **Ask** students to think of other words for the word part being discussed. For example, for *dis-* students might suggest: *disagree, disappear, disable,* and *disconnect.*

Apply and Assess

Students can work independently, in pairs, or in groups. Present sentences from text students are reading that contain compound words or words with affixes or endings. Have students write the word, its base word, the word part, and tell what the word means. Bring the group back together to share their findings.

If available, you may want to use any or all of these products for more word-study practice: the Grade 3 *Phonics Sourcebook,* Grade 3 *Phonemic Awareness and Phonics Manipulatives Kit, AstroWord* (Discs B and C), *Daily Word Routines Flip Chart.*

Strategy Routine for Fluency

Reread Familiar Text to Develop Fluency

About the Strategy

Fluent readers are able to decode text automatically, and as a result they can focus on meaning, develop greater confidence, and enjoy reading more.

How to Use the Strategy

1 **Write** on the board or on an overhead the following routine. Have students copy it to refer to later.
   a. Preview your reading and decide how to pronounce proper nouns.
   b. Practice reading difficult words so you read them more smoothly.
   c. Check pronunciations in a dictionary.
   d. Use punctuation correctly. Pause at commas. Let your voice rise and fall with end punctuation.
   e. Match your tone of voice to the tone of the piece.
   f. Use appropriate phrasing to build excitement or add emphasis.

2 **Help** students select a passage from a familiar story.

3 **Model** reading the passage aloud showing how a fluent reader sounds.

4 **Discuss** each point with students and demonstrate how to follow the routine.

Apply and Assess

Allow time for students to practice reading. Direct them to read the passage several times as they focus on the routine. Listen to students read aloud. Students can read to a partner or a small group. Allow students to use the fluency routine to critique each other on how well the selection was read.

If available, you may want to use *Leveled Readers A* or *B* for a fluency check.

© Scott Foresman 3

Word

Association or Symbol

Predicted definition: _____

One good sentence:

_____

_____

_____

_____

Verified definition:

_____

_____

_____

Another good sentence:

_____

_____

_____

_____

Title _____

Read the title and look at the pictures in the story.
What do you think a problem in the story might be?

I think a problem might be _____

_____

_____

After reading _____,
draw a picture of one of the problems in the story.

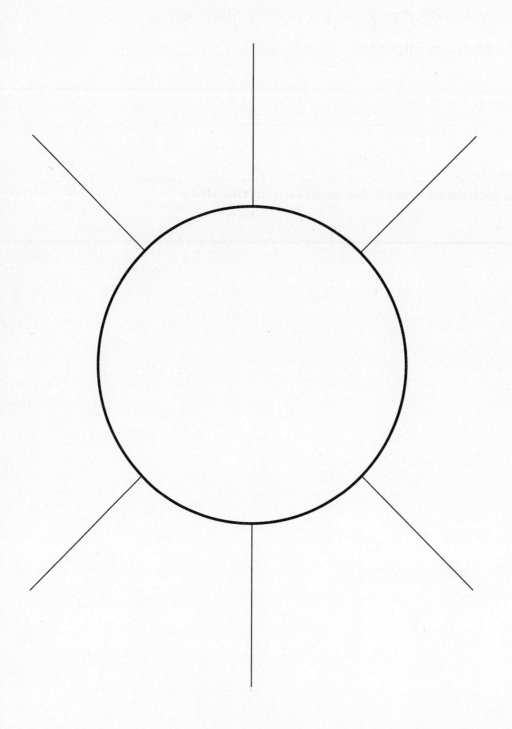

Topic _____

What We **K** now	What We **W** ant to Know	What We **L** earned

Title _____

> **Beginning**

> **Middle**

> **End**

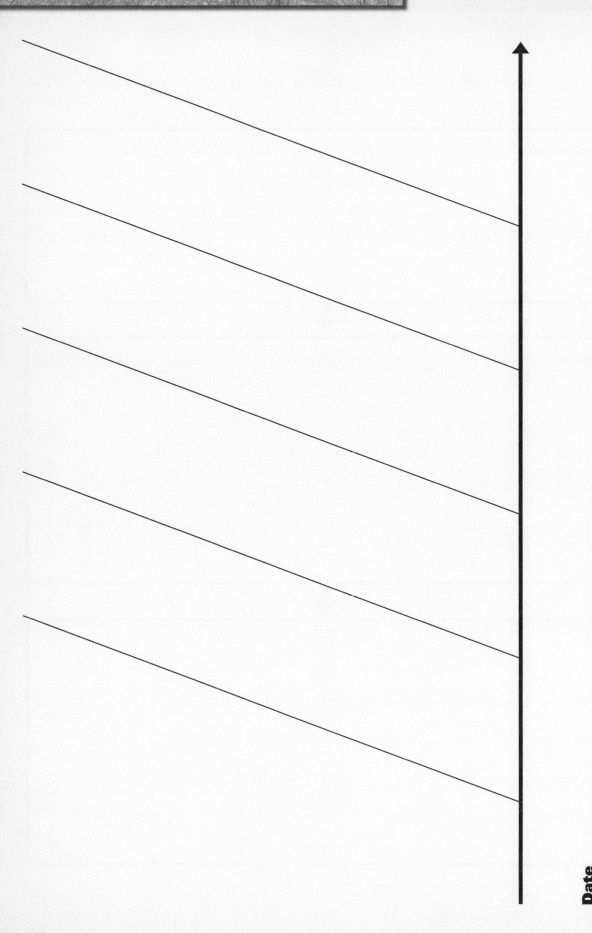

Date

Title _____

This story is about _____

_____
(name the characters)

This story takes place _____

_____
(where and when)

The action begins when _____

_____

_____

Then, _____

_____

Next, _____

_____

After that, _____

_____

The story ends when _____

_____

_____

Theme: _____

© Scott Foresman 3

Cause   **Effect**

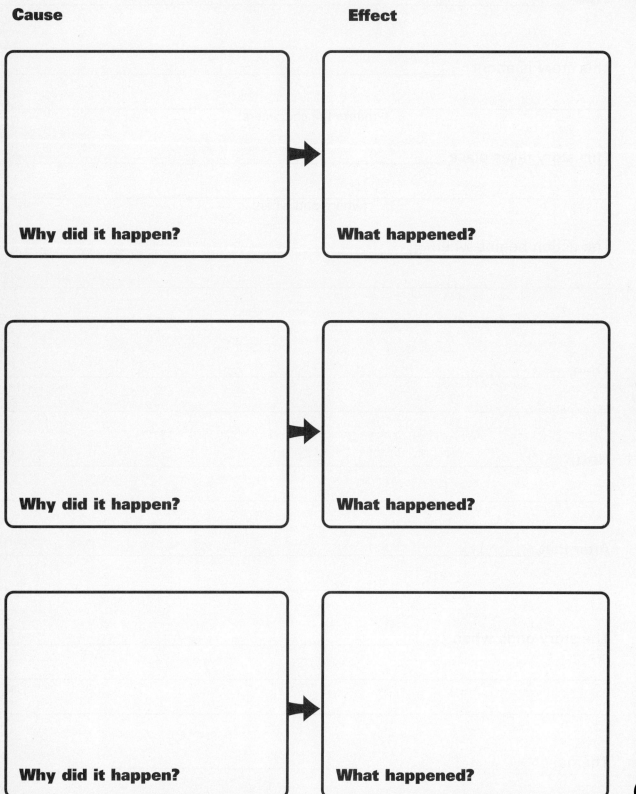

Why did it happen?   What happened?

Why did it happen?   What happened?

Why did it happen?   What happened?

Problem

Solution

Five-Column Chart

About Section Two of This Handbook

This section of the *Scott Foresman Reading Intervention Handbook* contains text and instruction designed to provide extra support for the struggling reader. It is important for all students to experience successful and meaningful reading. Providing students with reading materials that are at an appropriate instructional level and that students *want* to read is the first step toward developing fluent readers.

Students who are not able to read the main selections in the Student Edition will be able to read the Selection Summaries included in this handbook. The summaries will allow struggling students to participate in the same discussions and instruction as their classmates.

This section of the handbook also includes easy-to-follow teaching notes for the Selection Summaries and for the stories in *Collection for Readers*. These lessons provide the kinds of predictable routines that struggling readers need and that make learning possible.

You may want to follow the plan below with students who cannot read the main selection and who will read the Selection Summaries and the stories in *Collection for Readers* instead. (See the weekly 5-Day Planner in the Teacher's Edition for selection-specific information.)

Day 1   Include students in the Skill Lesson, Activate Prior Knowledge, and Introduce Vocabulary with the rest of the class.

Day 2   Have students read the selection summary and answer the "What Do You Think?" questions while their classmates read the main selection.

Day 3   Let students listen to the main selection on audiotape while their classmates finish the main selection. For additional instruction on the target comprehension skill introduced in the Skill Lesson on Day 1, students should listen to the Reteach Lesson following the main selection on the audiotape. Include students in Reader Response about the main selection.

Day 4 / 5 Have students read and discuss the related selection from *Collection for Readers.*

© Scott Foresman 3

Selection Summaries

Selection Summaries for every main selection in the Student Edition are included to provide scaffolding for students reading significantly below grade level. Selection summaries are written for students who are reading so far below grade level that they cannot read the main selection. The summaries allow students to be part of class discussions and instruction whenever possible.

Selection Summaries

- focus on story concepts that are central to meaning.

- retell, or summarize, the main selection in the core program.

- include related vocabulary and tested vocabulary words from the main selection, when appropriate.

- provide three response questions that focus on critical thinking, vocabulary, and making connections to the main selection.

- begin with a motivating question to invite students to read further.

- are provided in this handbook in blackline master form.

Collection for Readers

Collection for Readers is an anthology of selections designed to provide additional alternate text for students reading significantly below grade level. These very easy leveled readers are written two grades below grade level. Research shows that struggling readers need to read more, but unfortunately, they often end up reading less. *Collection for Readers* provides a mix of fiction and nonfiction text and is designed to be appealing to students.

The selections in *Collection for Readers*

- **are written two grade levels below** each main selection and increase in difficulty to parallel the main selections in the Student Edition.

- **support vocabulary development** through systematic repetition of high-frequency words and introduction of selection vocabulary.

- **enhance comprehension** of each selection with three response questions in *Collection for Readers.*
  Question 1 provides a graphic organizer for the purpose of understanding text/story structure.
  Question 2 practices 1 of 5 identified comprehension skills.
  Question 3 practices critical thinking skills.

- **are a source for Guided Reading.**

- **provide high-interest text that is thematically-related or topically-related to the main selections** in the Student Edition.

Lesson plans for teaching the selections in the *Collection for Readers* are available in this handbook: for fiction, see pages 76-77; for nonfiction, see pages 78-79. Also see pages 86–93 of this handbook for a list of the vocabulary words, high-frequency words, and comprehension skills practiced in *Collection for Readers* for this grade.

The *Collection for Readers* is also available in a Take-Home version. These blackline masters allow students to practice reading each selection as an individual reader at home. The Take-Home version also has blackline masters of the key graphic organizers that accompany the selections.

Skills in Collection for Readers

Text/Story Structure

Question 1 after every selection in *Collection for Readers* provides a **graphic organizer in the student book.** Students can copy the graphic organizer onto a piece of paper, or you can provide them with a blackline master, available in the *Collection for Readers* Take-Home version. Question 1 offers these students the opportunity to routinely practice identifying the text or story structure before they answer other comprehension questions. These structures include:

- **cause and effect**
- **compare and contrast**
- **main idea and supporting details**
- **plot/sequence of events**
- **problem/solution**

Comprehension Skills

Support for comprehension skill instruction is provided with the graphic organizers found in the Take-Home version of the *Collection for Readers* and the lesson plans for *Collection for Readers,* pages 76-79. After every selection in *Collection for Readers,* Question 2 will ask students to practice one of five key comprehension skills. These are the key skills that students frequently struggle with on state and national standardized tests.

These key comprehension skills are

- **main idea and details**
- **sequence**
- **drawing conclusions**
- **cause and effect**
- **compare and contrast**

What Are Selection Summaries?

As part of its Intervention Handbook, *Scott Foresman Reading* provides summaries of each main selection from the Student Edition. The Selection Summaries provide text for students who are reading significantly below level and are unable to read the main selection. The goal of the Selection Summaries is to provide extra support so that struggling readers are better prepared to join on-level readers in group discussions and response activities pertaining to the main selection.

How Do the Summaries Assist Struggling Readers?

Because the summaries are written below grade level, they are more accessible to struggling readers. These simple retellings of the main selection from the Student Edition help students succeed in the core reading program by focusing on story concepts and vocabulary at the struggling reader's level.

The easy readability of the summaries makes it possible for students to engage in routine rereading, which is key to reading success. Because the number of words students read is critical to developing fluency, it is vital that struggling readers read more, not less. For this reason, rereading should be emphasized.

Teaching Notes

Activate Prior Knowledge Include struggling readers when you activate prior knowledge and introduce vocabulary prior to the main selection in the Student Edition. If appropriate, you may want to include struggling readers when you teach the Skill Lesson in the Student Edition as well. Whenever possible it is important to include struggling readers in the instruction their classmates receive.

Motivate and Read To spark students' interest, each summary begins with a motivating question that is tied to the selection concepts. Use the motivating question to introduce the summary and to help students set purposes for reading. Ask them if the motivating question makes them curious about what they are about to read. Ask if there are any questions they want to add before they begin reading. Students can write their questions.

Give students an opportunity to make connections to the concepts introduced during background-building with the class. Have students make predictions about the selection. Question what they think the story will be about. Then have students read the Selection Summary while classmates read the main selection.

© Scott Foresman 3

Concept Development Each summary also includes three questions in "What Do You Think?" The first question asks students to think about what they've read and to draw upon their own experiences to help them develop an understanding of important selection concepts. Talking with students about the meaning of the text helps them develop strategies they can use when they read and respond to other selections. Struggling readers must be given the opportunity to talk about what they read—before, during, and after reading. Book talk is an important step in helping the student develop into a confident reader. Therefore, these questions sometimes prompt students to share their thoughts and ideas with friends or family members.

Vocabulary The second question focuses on vocabulary development. In all cases, the vocabulary words included here are central to the understanding of the summary. Tested vocabulary words from the main selection are used in the summaries so that students can develop vocabulary knowledge using the same words as their classmates.

Sometimes the vocabulary question asks the reader to find a particular word in the summary based on a simple definition. Then students are asked to relate the word to their own knowledge, ideas, or experiences and create an illustration that shows their understanding of the word. Other times the vocabulary question asks readers to retell what they've read using specific words from the summary. Occasionally they are asked to illustrate an important scene from the retelling.

Connect to the Main Selection Once students have read the summary, they should listen to the selection audio (if available) and follow along in the Student Edition. The final "What Do You Think?" question is intended to help readers think beyond the summary and make connections to the main selection based on their listening. If students were included in the instruction for the Skill Lesson with classmates, you may want to have them listen to the Reteach Lesson following the main selection on the audiotape to apply the same target comprehension skill. An answer key for all "What Do You Think?" questions can be found on pages 70-75 of this book.

Students who have read the selection summary (and listened to the main selection on audiotape) should participate in Reader Response following classmates' completion of the main selection.

© Scott Foresman 3

How I Spent My Summer Vacation

In school, Wallace Bleff told a story about his summer vacation. He said his mom and dad sent him to visit his Aunt Fern. Aunt Fern lived out west. His parents said Wallace's imagination was getting too wild. He needed a rest.

Wallace said cowboys captured him on the way to Aunt Fern's. They took him to their camp. One cowboy asked Wallace to be a cowboy. Wallace said yes. He wrote to his Aunt Fern to let her know where he was.

Wallace stayed with the cowboys. He got a cowboy hat and pants. He learned how to ride and rope and make fire with sticks.

Then Aunt Fern called. "Bring the cowboys over," she said. Aunt Fern had lots of good food and a band played music.

Then Wallace saw something terrible. A lot of big cattle were running at them. It was scary. Wallace saw a red cloth. He waved the red cloth in front of the cattle. The cattle were scared. They ran away. The cowboys cheered. They said Wallace was a "true buckaroo."

What Do You Think?

1. Is this a true story? Was Wallace really a cowboy? Do you think he made up the story?

2. Retell the story using the words below. Draw a picture of what you would do if cattle were running at a group of people.

cowboys   **cattle**   **west**

3. Did you listen to the story on tape? If so, what did the cowboys do after Wallace frightened the cattle away?

© Scott Foresman 3

Goldilocks helps herself to whatever she wants.
Read about what happens to her.

Goldilocks and the Three Bears

Goldilocks went to the three bears' house. Papa Bear, Mama Bear, and Baby Bear were not home. Goldilocks walked right in. She saw three bowls of porridge. She tasted each one. Papa Bear's was too hot. Mama Bear's was too cold. Baby Bear's was just right. Goldilocks gobbled it up.

Goldilocks went into a different room. She saw three rocking chairs. She sat in each one. Papa Bear's chair was too hard. Mama Bear's chair was too soft. Baby Bear's chair was just right. Goldilocks rocked and rocked, and the chair broke.

Goldilocks now wanted a comfortable place to nap. She found three beds. Goldilocks did not like two of the beds. She tried the little bed. It was just right. She fell asleep.

The three hungry bears came home. They were surprised! Baby Bear's breakfast was gone, his chair was broken, and somebody was sleeping in his bed. Goldilocks woke up. She jumped out the window and ran home. The three bears never saw her again.

What Do You Think?

1. Think about what Goldilocks did. What does this tell you about her?

2. Retell the story using the words below. Draw a picture of the three bears when they find Goldilocks.

gobbled   **rocking chair**   **comfortable**

3. Did you listen to the story on tape? If so, what was Papa Bear like?

Anthony Reynoso: Born to Rope

Anthony Reynoso ropes and rides Mexican Rodeo style with his father and grandfather. It is a tradition. Anthony's grandfather showed Anthony's dad how to do it. Now, Anthony learns from his dad.

At school, Anthony does not think about roping and riding. But after school, he and his dad practice for shows. Anthony also does activities like other kids. He does his homework, collects basketball cards, and shoots baskets with his dad.

There is a big show on Saturday. Anthony helps prepare the ropes before the show. At the show, Anthony is nervous. His dad goes first. Then it's Anthony's turn. Anthony does a trick even his dad can't do. He puts a rope in his teeth and spins it. Anthony feels like a star when tourists at the show want to take pictures with him. But Anthony's mom is his biggest fan. She is going to have a baby soon. Anthony will show the baby how to rope.

What Do You Think?

1. Compare what Anthony does to what other kids might do. What activity does he do that might be different?

2. Find the word that means "to do something again and again." Have you ever had to do something again and again, such as play an instrument, to get it right? Explain. Draw a picture of what you did.

3. Did you listen to the selection on tape? If so, what activities does Anthony do with his family that other families might do too?

How does Herbie trick Annabelle?
Read to find out how they feel about each other.

Herbie and Annabelle

Annabelle Hodgekiss had the chicken pox. Herbie's teacher had him bring get-well cards to her home. Mr. Hodgekiss answered the door. He asked Herbie to give Annabelle the cards himself. Herbie knew that Annabelle was mad at him. The last thing he wanted was to see her!

Luckily, he didn't have to. She was hiding under a sheet! She didn't want anybody to see her spots. She couldn't see who Herbie was. She thought he was her friend John. So Herbie pretended to be John. He read Annabelle some get-well cards. She did not like the first card. Herbie read a poem from the second card. Annabelle giggled. She said, "That's funny! Who wrote it?" It was from Herbie. Annabelle was surprised. Annabelle explained why she was mad at Herbie.

Still Annabelle said, "Herbie Jones does have a way with words." Then she warned her visitor not to tell Herbie what she had said. Herbie agreed not to tell. As Herbie walked home, he thought about what Annabelle had said. Maybe he did have a way with words. Herbie made up a few new poems as he walked home.

What Do You Think?

1. How is Herbie able to make Annabelle think he is John? What do you think of Herbie doing this?

2. Find the word that means "made believe." Have you ever made believe you were somebody else? Explain. Draw a picture of yourself when you made believe you were somebody else.

3. Did you listen to the story on tape? If so, would you be mad at Herbie for some of the things Annabelle said he did? Why or why not?

Allie's Basketball Dream

Allie's father gave her a basketball. It was something she really wanted. Allie took her basketball and went to the playground with her father. She found a court to practice on. Allie took two shots and missed. Some boys playing basketball in the next court laughed.

Allie tried to get her friends to play basketball, but they wouldn't. One friend said that basketball was a boy's game. Another friend wouldn't shoot baskets with a girl. Allie kept shooting and missing. The boys in the next court laughed again. Allie sat down.

Then Buddy came by. Allie had seen him jumping rope with girls. He wanted to trade Allie for her basketball. She wouldn't. Buddy told Allie that some boys think girls shouldn't play basketball. Allie said, "That's dumb. Some girls think boys shouldn't be jumping rope. That's dumb too."

Allie was determined to make a shot. She tried again. The shot went in! She tried a few more times. Another shot went in! The boys in the next court clapped. Allie heard her father say, "Hooray for Allie!"

What Do You Think?

1. Think about how many times Allie tries to make a basket. What does that tell you about her?

2. Retell the story using the words below. Draw a picture to show how you think Allie looked after she finally made a basket.

   basketball   **playground**   **shot**   **court**

3. Did you listen to the story on tape? If so, how do you think Allie acted toward the boys who laughed?

Some plants eat animals! How do they do it?

Fly Traps! Plants That Bite Back

The narrator who told this story liked to watch plants eat animals. Plants that eat animals are called carnivorous plants. They grow all around the world. Each has different ways to trap animals. The narrator traveled everywhere to find them.

He found the bladderwort plant with its trap door. When insects land near the trap door it opens. In goes the bug! The narrator looked for a bigger plant—a sundew plant. The sundew uses sticky leaves to catch insects. But the narrator wanted an even bigger plant. He grew a Venus flytrap. Its leaves snap close when bugs land on it.

The narrator got a cobra lily next. When bugs crawl inside this plant's leaves, they cannot climb out. The narrator thought this was the biggest plant. It wasn't.

He traveled far away to find a pitcher plant. The pitcher plant's leaves look like vases. Tree frogs and spiders can live inside. But there was still a bigger plant. One that eats squirrels! The narrator said one day he would go see it.

What Do You Think?

1. What are the different ways the plants trap animals? Tell a friend about these plants.

2. Retell the selection using the words below. Make up your own plant that eats insects. Draw how it looks.

    plants   **insects**   **trap**

3. Did you listen to the selection on tape? If so, what are some of the words the narrator uses to describe the plants?

© Scott Foresman 3

What happens when a kid meets some guys from space? Could it really happen?

Guys from Space

One day, some guys from space landed in a kid's backyard. They asked the kid to go for a ride. The kid asked his mother. "Sure," said his mom. She didn't even want to see the space guys. The space guys would not let the kid aboard the spaceship until he had a space helmet. He used his dog's water bowl as his helmet. Off they all flew to another planet.

They got there very fast. The space guys did not know anything about the planet. They all explored the planet. The kid found a rock that talked! The rock told the space guys how to get to a root beer stand. The space guys liked root beer! They ordered some root beer and paid with plastic fish because plastic fish is what they use for money on their planet. The root beer had ice cream in it.

The space guys never had root beer with ice cream in it before. They liked it a lot. They liked it so much that they wanted to rush back to their planet to tell everybody. They said ice cream in root beer would make them heroes! They dropped the kid back on Earth and said good-bye. The kid told his mother about his trip. She said, "That's nice, dear."

What Do You Think?

1. Do you think the kid traveled to a place that could be real? Explain.

2. Find the word in the story that is the name of a drink. Have you ever had this drink? Draw a picture of the space guys drinking it.

3. Did you listen to the story on tape? If so, do you think the space guys acted like real people? What did they do to make you think so?

What happens in a tornado?
Read to learn why they are so powerful.

Tornado Alert

Tornadoes are powerful storms. They happen when cold air meets warm air. They form funnels that touch the ground. It gets dark during a tornado. There is thunder and lightning, rain and hail. The thunder and wind make a lot of noise.

Tornadoes can happen anywhere. They cause damage because they pick up things, such as branches and bricks. They rip off roofs and leave wrecked houses. Scientists use special equipment to find tornadoes. Some people look for tornadoes. These people are called tornado spotters. They tell radio and television stations to send out warnings so people will know a tornado is coming. Then people can go to a safe spot.

A safe spot during a tornado is a storm cellar. A storm cellar is an underground room with heavy doors. Another safe spot is a basement. People should not go by glass windows during a tornado. If they are outside, they should find a ditch and lie down. People can be safe from a tornado if they know what to do.

What Do You Think?

1. What did you learn? Have you ever heard about tornadoes?

2. Retell the selection using the words below. Draw a picture of what you think a tornado looks like.

   powerful   **storm**   **wind**   **noise**

3. Did you listen to the selection on tape? If so, what other safety tips can you add?

© Scott Foresman 3

Danger—Icebergs!

Icebergs are big pieces of ice that float in the ocean. They are found in very cold places. Some icebergs look like mountains or buildings. Some are wide and flat.

Icebergs move slowly. You can walk faster than many icebergs move! Icebergs float to warm water where they melt. But it can take three to four years before they melt away.

Icebergs are dangerous for boats. Boats stay away from icebergs because they can sink if they hit one. It is hard to see icebergs. That is because most of an iceberg is hidden below the water.

Long ago, sailors kept watch day and night so they wouldn't hit an iceberg. They did not have telescopes or radios to help guide them. The most famous boat to sink because of an iceberg was the *Titanic* in 1912. People thought nothing could sink the ship. It was the biggest ship ever built at that time.

Today, ships have better equipment to see icebergs. Airplanes, radar, satellites, and the coast guard are used to alert ships of icebergs.

What Do You Think?

1. Why is an iceberg hard to see? Why does that make it dangerous?

2. Retell the story using the words below. Draw a picture of how you think it looks when a ship hits an iceberg.

dangerous   **alert**   **sink**

3. Did you listen to the selection on tape? If so, what else did the author describe?

How do Halla and her friends rescue pufflings?
Read about these chicks.

Nights of the Pufflings

Halla watches the puffins return. She lives on an island in Iceland where puffins come each summer to lay their eggs. Puffins are birds that live at sea. They come ashore only during the summer to lay eggs in the cliffs. Halla and her friends can't wait to see the pufflings!

When the pufflings hatch, older birds fly out to sea to catch fish for them. Halla and her friends never see the chicks, but they hear them calling for food. By August, the chicks are ready to fly out to the sea. They fly at night. Some birds get confused by the village lights and get lost. They do not make it to the water.

Halla and her friends help rescue the stranded pufflings. If they didn't, other animals might get them. Cars could also run them over. The pufflings are kept in cardboard boxes until morning. Then, Halla and her friends go to the beach and set the pufflings free. Halla says good-bye to the puffins until next year.

What Do You Think?

1. What happens once the eggs hatch? Tell a friend about how you would help to save the pufflings.

2. Find the word that means "to save something." Have you ever saved something or seen somebody save something? Explain.

3. Did you listen to the selection on tape? If so, what else did Halla and her friends do when trying to save the pufflings?

Selection Summary **49**

What does it take to write a book?
Read about the steps authors take to do it.

What Do Authors Do?

What Do Authors Do? is about how writers get ideas and get their books published. After seeing their cat and dog chase each other, two writers each get a different idea for a book. It's difficult to write. One writer makes notes and outlines what he thinks might happen in the story. The other writer draws pictures to help her with her idea. Most authors do research. They read books, newspapers, and letters. Each takes notes. They talk to people and listen to people. Then they write and rewrite. Authors work hard.

Authors read their stories to their families and friends. They get suggestions. When authors get stuck they take a break until they aren't stuck anymore. Authors who draw pictures for their books make a sample to show how the book might look.

It can take a long time to write a book. When it's finished, authors send their books to publishers. Then they wait a long time to hear if the publisher liked the book. When a rejection letter comes, authors don't give up. They rewrite their book and send it to other publishers until it gets published.

What Do You Think?

1. Think about the steps in the story. Have you ever had to follow steps to do something, such as your homework? What were the steps?

2. Retell the selection using the words below. Do you have an idea for a story? Draw a picture about it.

   authors   **difficult**   **publish**   **suggestions**

3. Did you listen to the selection on tape? If so, how do the authors get information for writing their books?

© Scott Foresman 3

Tops and Bottoms

Bear was lazy. He had a lot of money and land. But he just wanted to sleep. Hare was clever, but he had lost his land because of a bet. His family was hungry. He had to do something. Hare and his wife came up with a plan. Hare asked Bear if he could plant crops in a field by Bear's house. Hare said he would do all the hard work. Bear only had to choose—tops or bottoms? Bear chose tops.

Hare worked. Bear slept. At harvest time, Hare's family dug up carrots, radishes, and beets. Bear got the tops. Hare kept the bottoms. "Hare, all the best parts are in your half," said Bear. It was a trick! Bear told Hare to plant the crops again. He wanted the bottoms.

Hare worked. Bear slept. At harvest time, Hare's family picked lettuce, broccoli, and celery. Bear got the bottoms. Hare kept the tops. He had tricked Bear twice! Hare had to plant the crops again. Bear wanted the tops and the bottoms. So, Hare planted corn. Bear got the tops and the bottoms. Hare kept the corn in the middle. That was it! Bear said he would plant his own crops. And he did. He stopped sleeping all of the time. Hare's family opened a vegetable stand.

What Do You Think?

1. Did you know Hare was going to trick Bear? If so, why? Explain.

2. Retell the story using the words below. Draw somebody being lazy.

   lazy   **trick**   **clever**   **crops**

3. Did you listen to the story on tape? If so, what did you learn about Bear?

© Scott Foresman 3

Will Ursula become part of the family? Read about how a family grows to love their mom's new Seeing Eye dog.

Mom's Best Friend

After Marit died, Mom got another Seeing Eye dog to guide her. Mom had to go to the Seeing Eye school to train with her new dog, Ursula. I was worried that I wouldn't love Ursula the way I loved Marit. But when Mom arrived home with Ursula, I was crazy about her.

Then I wondered if Ursula would love me. I tried to be patient while Mom trained Ursula. Mom taught her the different routes in our neighborhood. Ursula learned to cross streets and how to find her way home. She became Mom's shadow. She was right there when Mom showered or slept. Mom and Ursula had to form an attachment. My brother, Dad, and I could only watch while Mom and Ursula played.

Once Mom and Ursula could get around easily, Mom taught her how to stay home alone. She didn't bark or chew on furniture. Finally, it was our turn to play with Ursula. She liked us! I think Ursula is the best dog in the world.

What Do You Think?

1. Why do you think it's important for Mom and Ursula to spend a lot of time together before the rest of the family can play with Ursula?

2. Find the word that means to "lead or show someone the way." Have you ever helped to lead or show somebody around? Explain. Draw a picture that shows leading someone.

3. Did you listen to the selection on tape? If so, do you think Ursula liked the family when she first met them?

Will fear stop Spider from joining the spelling bee? Read about how he faces his fear.

Brave as a Mountain Lion

Spider doesn't want to be in the spelling bee. He is afraid to stand up in front of people. Dad tells him that he was scared to be in a spelling bee too. So he pretended to be a brave animal. Later, Spider looks at a painting of a mountain lion. "Brave as a mountain lion," he says to himself.

The next day, Spider's fear has not gone away. His grandmother tells him to try to be as clever as a coyote. Still, Spider is afraid. He decides not to be in the contest.

Then his brother tells him his secret for not feeling scared. It was to be silent.

Spider watches a little spider spin a web. She is silent. The spider bravely drops down into space with nothing to hang on to. She cleverly weaves a web from nothing. The spider is silent, but Spider feels her speak. She tells him to listen to his spirit and not to be afraid. Spider decides to be in the contest! He bravely goes on stage, he cleverly turns his back to the crowd, and silently he listens to his spirit. When it's all over, Spider finishes second, and his family is proud.

What Do You Think?

1. Think about the decision Spider has to make. What do you think helps him finally face his fear?

2. Find the word that means to "showing courage." Have you ever done something that took courage? Explain.

3. Did you listen to the story on tape? If so, why do you think Spider went to the gym to see where the spelling bee was going to be held?

Your Dad Was Just Like You

Peter wanted to move in with Grandpa. Dad was mad at him again. This time Peter was running around and he broke something purple on Dad's dresser. Peter told Grandpa that his dad never smiled; he only yelled. Grandpa said, "When he was a boy, your dad was just like you." He laughed and smiled all the time. He told knock-knock jokes and played basketball. But what he loved to do most was run!

Peter's dad was in a big race once. He really wanted to win it. He had something to prove. It began to rain seconds before the race. Peter's dad did not run for cover like the other kids. He ran to the finish. Nobody was there to congratulate him or give him a trophy. He cried. Grandpa made him a trophy. The same purple trophy that Peter had broken!

Grandpa said he used to fight a lot with Peter's dad, but everything changed the day of the race. Peter went home. He fixed the purple trophy and gave it to his dad.

What Do You Think?

1. Do you think Peter finally understands his father at the end of the story? Why or why not?

2. Find the word that means to "show that something is true." Have you ever tried to do this for something you knew or thought was true? Explain.

3. Did you listen to the story on tape? If so, why did Peter's dad feel he had to prove himself by winning the race?

© Scott Foresman 3

Ananse the Spider didn't like to share.
Read how Akye the Turtle repays Ananse for being greedy.

Ananse's Feast

Ananse the Spider was clever. Before the drought, he stored away food. Now he was the only one who had much to eat. Ananse decided to have a feast. But he didn't want to share it. Akye the Turtle was hungry and stopped by Ananse's house to get something to eat.

Ananse could not send Akye away, so he invited him to be his guest. Akye was amazed at Ananse's pile of food. Ananse insisted that Akye wash his hands before he ate. Ah, but this was a trick! As poor Akye washed by the river, Ananse ate all of the food. Akye just smiled, thanked him, and said he hoped to repay him some day.

The drought ended. It rained hard. Ananse had little to eat now. Akye invited him to a feast under the river. Ananse, delighted, wore a brilliant ceremonial robe. He put pebbles in the pockets to help him sink to the river's bottom. Akye asked him to remove his robe. Ah, this was a trick! As soon as Anansi removed the robe, he floated to the surface without a bit of food to eat.

What Do You Think?

1. Think about how Ananse and Akye act in the story. Do you think they treat each other fairly?

2. Retell the story using the words below. Draw the most important scene from your retelling of the story.

   brilliant   **delighted**   **feast**   **guest**

3. Did you listen to the story on tape? If so, remember how Akye told Ananse that it was only good manners to remove his robe before eating. Would you have taken off the robe?

What will Sam do with his lucky money?
Will he spend it or give it away?

Sam and the Lucky Money

Sam went with his mother to Chinatown for New Year's Day. His grandparents gave him four crisp dollar bills in small red envelopes called *leisees*. He could spend the lucky money on whatever he wanted. The streets in Chinatown were crowded. Sam was startled when he saw an old man in dirty clothing, not wearing any shoes. "Bare feet in winter!" Sam thought. "Where are his shoes?"

Sam and his mother went to a bakery. He thought about buying buns and cookies, but he remembered the old man. He decided he wasn't hungry. Then they went to a toy store. A basketball would be the perfect way to spend his lucky money. Sam got angry because he didn't have enough money to buy it. His mother scolded him and said he should appreciate it when someone gave him something.

Sam saw the old man again. This time he gave the man his lucky money and told him to buy socks for his feet. As he headed home, Sam knew he was the lucky one.

What Do You Think?

1. Think about when and where the story takes place. What time of the year is it? Where are Sam and his mother?

2. Find the word that means "having or bringing good luck." Have you ever had good luck? Explain.

3. Did you listen to the story on tape? If so, would you like to visit Chinatown? Why or why not?

A storm's coming. Is it the best time to bake a cake? Read how a girl overcomes her fear of thunder with help from her grandma.

Thunder Cake

I hid under the bed when I heard the thunder. Grandma said it was Thunder Cake baking weather. She told me not to be afraid of the thunder. When I saw the lightning, I started counting. When I heard the thunder, I stopped counting. Grandma said that the number I counted told us how many miles away the storm was.

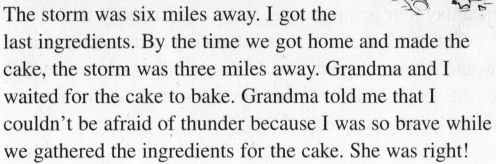

We went to the barn to get eggs from mean Nellie Peck Hen. I was scared. The lightning flashed. The storm was nine miles away. We got milk from Kick Cow and then went to the dry shed to get chocolate, sugar, and flour. I was scared as we walked the path through the woods. The storm was six miles away. I got the last ingredients. By the time we got home and made the cake, the storm was three miles away. Grandma and I waited for the cake to bake. Grandma told me that I couldn't be afraid of thunder because I was so brave while we gathered the ingredients for the cake. She was right!

What Do You Think?

1. How does the girl feel at the beginning of the story? Does she change her mind about how she feels by the end of the story?

2. Retell the story using the words below. Draw the most important scene from your retelling of the story.

   thunder   **lightning**   **weather**

3. Did you listen to the story on tape? If so, how does Grandma help the girl stop being afraid of the thunder?

One Grain of Rice

Long ago in India, a royal raja, or king, stored rice for the people in his village. The raja said he would keep the rice so that during a famine no one would be hungry.

Each year, the raja received most of the people's rice. The people were left with just enough rice to get by. Then one year there was a famine. The raja did not give the rice to the people as he had promised. Instead, he had a feast for himself.

A village girl made a plan. She has seen some rice fall out of a basket. She brought the rice to the raja. He wished to reward her. The clever girl asked for a single grain of rice. She asked the raja to double the rice each day for thirty days.

"Tomorrow you will give me two grains of rice, the next day four grains of rice, and so on for thirty days."

The raja did not think the doubling of one grain of rice would add up to much rice. In the end, the girl received all of the people's rice that the raja had stored. She returned it to the hungry people.

What Do You Think?

1. How does the raja treat the people in his village? How does this compare to the way the girl treats the people in the village?

2. Find the word that means "give something good for something done." Draw a picture to show when this happens to the girl.

3. Did you listen to the story on tape? If so, do you think the raja learned a lesson? Why?

© Scott Foresman 3

People were afraid of Lucia Zenteno.
Read why people treated her badly.

The Woman Who Outshone the Sun

No one knew where Lucia Zenteno came from. She was beautiful and had long, black, flowing hair. Nothing shone as brightly as Lucia, not even the sun. The river she bathed in fell in love with her. All the water, fishes, and otters would flow through her hair. She would comb them out, and they would return to the river.

People were afraid of Lucia because she was different. They called her cruel names even though the elders told them not to. Lucia was not mean in return. Her quiet dignity angered some people. They drove her from the village. But the river would not let Lucia leave alone. The water, fishes, and otters went with her. The people were left to suffer from thirst.

After time, the people searched for Lucia to ask for forgiveness. "I will ask the river to return to you," she said. She told them that they would have to treat everyone with kindness, even those who seemed different from them.

What Do You Think?

1. What was Lucia like? Would you be afraid of her? Why or why not? Discuss the story with your family.

2. Find the word that means "to have a dry feeling in your mouth caused by needing drink." Have you ever had this feeling? Explain.

3. Did you listen to the story on tape? If so, think about when Lucia asks the river to return to where it belonged. If you were Lucia, would you have helped the people? Why or why not?

Imagine being the first person to fly across the Atlantic Ocean without stopping. Read about Charles Lindbergh's flight.

Flight: The Journey of Charles Lindbergh

In 1927, Charles Lindbergh attempts to fly across the Atlantic Ocean from New York to Paris without stopping. He flies alone in a small plane. The trip is 3,600 miles. He leaves his radio and parachute behind, so he can carry an extra fuel tank. Will he have enough fuel to make the trip? He does not sleep the night before. He has waited his entire life to take this flight. Lindbergh follows the coastline, flying very close to the water.

When he can no longer see land, he must chart his course so he does not get lost. He is now 2,000 miles away from Paris. Lindbergh is very tired and almost falls asleep. He holds his eyelids open with his fingers. After many hours, he sees land. After 34 hours in the air, Lindbergh spots Paris. As he lands, he is greeted by thousands of people. He is the first person to fly from New York to Paris without stopping.

What Do You Think?

1. Think about Lindbergh's trip. Did anything make you think he might not make it to Paris?

2. Find the word that means "to take a trip in an aircraft." Have you ever taken or knew someone who has taken a trip in an aircraft? Explain. Draw a picture of Charles Lindbergh on his trip.

3. Did you listen to the selection on tape? If so, what do you think Lindbergh wrote in his diary the day after he landed in Paris? Do you think it was a good idea to keep a diary on the flight?

A duck family makes their home in downtown Tokyo, Japan.
What happens when it's time to move?

Chibi: A True Story from Japan

One morning, a mother duck laid her eggs in an office park in downtown Tokyo, Japan. She didn't care about the busy street close by. The ten eggs hatched, and the ducklings caused a sensation. Many people visited the park to see them and take pictures.

Mr. Sato, a newspaper reporter, named the tiniest duckling Chibi, which means "tiny." Chibi was everyone's favorite. She struggled to catch up with her brothers and sisters.

Then the duck family outgrew the pool at the park. The mother duck decided to lead her ducks across the busy street to the Emperor's Gardens. Newspaper reporters waited all night for the ducks to move. Everyone was prepared to help the ducks cross the street. But when the mother duck went in a different direction, Mr. Sato ran into the street to stop traffic. Luckily, the ducks made it safely to the Emperor's Gardens. All the ducks jumped right into the water. Chibi was afraid to jump. Finally, with one big splash she did it!

What Do You Think?

1. Compare Chibi to the other ducks. How is she different from them?

2. Find the word that means "young ducks." Have you ever seen young ducks? Explain. Draw a picture of young ducks.

3. Did you listen to the selection on tape? If so, use details from the selection to explain what Mr. Sato is like.

© Scott Foresman 3

Will a snowstorm stop Irene from delivering a dress to the duchess? How will Brave Irene make it through the storm?

Brave Irene

Irene's mother made a lovely dress for the duchess. The ball was that night, but she was too sick to deliver it. Irene said she would do it. It was very cold and snowy out. Irene packed the dress in a big box and left. The wind whirled the snow everywhere. It was hard for Irene to walk. "Go home!" the wind said. Irene thought about turning back, but she pressed on. The dress had to get to the duchess!

The wind wrestled Irene for the box. Brave Irene would not give it up. But the wind ripped the box open and carried the dress through the air until it disappeared. An upset Irene decided to take the empty box to the duchess to explain what happened. Then she stepped in a hole and hurt her ankle. Still, Irene kept going.

She finally made it to the palace. And, just outside the palace, she found the dress stuck to a tree. The duchess, pleased Irene had arrived, couldn't believe Irene had made it through the snow.

What Do You Think?

1. Where does the story take place? Would the story be different if the setting was a warm place?

2. Retell the story using the words below. Draw what you think it looked like when the box was ripped open and the dress was carried away.

   snow   **ripped**   **wind**   **whirled**

3. Did you listen to the story on tape? If so, imagine yourself in Irene's place. Would you do anything differently to get the dress to the duchess?

Have you ever wanted something badly?
Read about Booker's desire to learn to read.

More Than Anything Else

More than anything else, I want to learn to read. But now, I must work at the saltworks. Papa, my brother John, and I shovel salt all day. My arms ache from lifting the shovel, but I do not think about the pain. I think about reading. I know if I had a chance, I could learn.

It is night. We walk home. I see a man reading a newspaper aloud. I have found hope, and it is as brown as me. I see myself reading and knowing what the black marks mean. At home, I tell Mama I have to learn to read. She understands how I feel. One evening in our cabin, Mama gives me a book. A book she cannot read. But she says it's the alphabet. She thinks it's a song. After work, I study my book. I try to figure out the sounds of the marks.

I look for the newspaper man. He tells me the song and the sounds the marks make. I jump and laugh as I sing it. The man draws my name, Booker. I stare at the picture. I know I can hold it forever.

What Do You Think?

1. Do you think Booker will someday learn to read? What does he do to make you think so?

2. Find the word that means "a set of letters that represent sounds." Do you remember when you learned these letters? Explain.

3. Did you listen to the selection on tape? If so, do you think Booker has to work hard at his job? Have you ever had to do hard work like Booker does?

Leah's family is having hard times.
What does Leah give up to save her family's farm?

Leah's Pony

The year the corn grew tall, Leah's papa bought her a pony. Leah took very good care of the pony. The year the corn didn't grow, Papa sold the pigs and some cattle. "These are hard times," he told Leah.

Papa didn't have any corn to sell, so he couldn't pay the bank money he owed. He told Leah that the bank would have an auction to sell their things. Worst of all, they would sell the tractor. Without the tractor, Papa couldn't plant corn and they would have to leave the farm.

Leah wanted to help. On the day of the auction, she went to town. She sold her pony for a dollar. Then she went to the auction. She arrived just as Papa's best bull, Mama's prize rooster, and Leah's favorite calf were being sold. When it was time to auction the tractor, Leah bid one dollar. No one bid against her, and the tractor was hers. Then the people began bidding very low for the chickens and truck. They bought everything and gave them back to Leah's family. The next morning, Leah found her pony in the barn too.

What Do You Think?

1. Was it a good idea for Leah to sell her pony? Why or why not? What information in the story supports your opinion? Ask a friend if Leah should have sold her pony.

2. Retell the story using the words below. Draw a picture of what you think a farm auction looks like.

   pony   **auction**   **tractor**   **bid**

3. Did you listen to the story on tape? If so, do you think Leah could actually buy a tractor for only one dollar? Why is she able to buy it?

There are many steps to making a piñata.
How does Don Ricardo make his piñatas?

The Piñata Maker

Don Ricardo makes piñatas for parties. Today, he is making a swan. First, he makes paste from flour and water. He rolls banana leaves into a rod and wraps it with brown paper. Don Ricardo puts paste on the rod and makes an S-shape for the swan's neck. He dries it in the sun. When dry, he covers the neck with white paper. He makes the swan's tail from cardboard. To make the wings, he traces a pattern onto cardboard. Then he cuts two triangles for the beak, and he cuts out the feet. He makes the eyes from black letters he cuts from a bag. Don Ricardo uses a clay pot for the swan's body. He glues newspaper all over it. After he makes the feathers from crepe paper, he pastes the neck and tail onto the body. Then he paints the beak and feet. Finally, he puts on the wings. The piñata is ready for a fiesta.

What Do You Think?

1. Think about how to make a piñata. Do you paint the piñata before you make the paste? What kind of piñata would you make?

2. Retell what you read using the words below. Draw a picture of how you think the piñata looks after it is finished.

    swan   **make**   **paste**   **pattern**

3. Did you listen to the selection on tape? If so, do you think making piñatas would be hard? What do you like to make?

© Scott Foresman 3

Can you mail a little girl?
Read about May's train trip in a mail car.

Mailing May

May's parents promised to send her to Grandma's for a visit. But the ticket cost too much. May was very sad. So, her parents came up with a plan. Cousin Leonard worked in the mail car on the train. Pa and Leonard took May to the post office and asked the postmaster to mail May. There was nothing in the rule book that said they couldn't mail a little girl. He weighed May and glued some stamps to her coat, along with an address label.

May was ready for her adventure! She had never been on a train. The train went through mountains and tunnels. It crossed valleys. At one spot, the tracks twisted back and forth down the mountain. May felt dizzy. The cranky train conductor saw her. "That girl better have a ticket or money to buy one," he said to Leonard. The conductor laughed when Leonard showed him the stamps on May's coat. "I've seen everything now," he said.

May arrived at Grandma's house in time for lunch. Her parents had kept their promise.

What Do You Think?

1. Would the story have ended differently if the conductor made May pay for her ticket? Write an ending to the story in which the conductor makes May pay.

2. Retell the story using the words below. Draw a picture of how you would look if you were sent through the mail.

   mail   **label**   **conductor**

3. Did you listen to the story on tape? If so, what does May try to do to get money for her train ride?

© Scott Foresman 3

How easy is it for Ramona and Beezus to cook dinner?
Read about the mess the two make.

The Extra-Good Sunday

Ramona and Beezus complained about their mother's dinner the night before. As punishment, they had to make dinner on Sunday. The two sisters tried to be extra-good on Sunday, hoping their parents would forget about dinner. But they didn't forget. The sisters didn't find much in the refrigerator. They found chicken thighs and yogurt. At first, the two wanted to make something awful to get back at their parents. But they would have to eat it too.

So, the cooking began. The two pulled the skin off the chicken and left it on the counter. Ramona didn't have the ingredients to make cornbread. She used banana yogurt instead of buttermilk and Cream of Wheat when she ran out of cornmeal. The two not only made dinner, but they made a mess! They also realized how hard it was to cook. How did their mom do it? Ramona and Beezus were grateful when their parents enjoyed—or pretended to enjoy the meal.

What Do You Think?

1. Do you think Ramona and Beezus will ever complain about their mother's cooking again? Why or why not? Find examples in the story to support your opinion.

2. Retell the story using the words below. Draw the most important scene from your retelling of the story.

   complained   **punishment**   **refrigerator**   **ingredients**

3. Did you listen to the story on tape? If so, would you like to have to eat the meal Ramona and Beezus made? Write a menu for a meal you would make.

© Scott Foresman 3

Maxine takes a trip to space to complete her art project.
Read how she becomes the youngest astronaut ever!

Floating Home

Maxine's teacher gave her an art assignment. She had to look at her home in a new way and draw it. Maxine was going to draw the most unusual picture of all, a picture of Earth from space. She was going to be the youngest astronaut ever!

As she prepared to go into space, newspaper and television reporters asked her questions. "Maxine, why are you doing it?" they asked. "I'm doing it for art," Maxine said. She wore a pressure suit to protect her during liftoff. She had everything she needed for an emergency. During the launch, everything shook, and it was noisy. The shuttle traveled faster and faster. Then the rocket boosters were released. The acceleration pressed Maxine into her seat. She couldn't move. Suddenly, everything changed. Maxine felt herself floating. She was in space! She looked out the window for her house but realized that her home was one big Earth.

What Do You Think?

1. Do you think Maxine wanted to do well on her project? Why or why not?

2. Retell the story using the words below. Include yourself in the story. Draw a picture of yourself taking a ride in space.

   astronaut   **emergency**   **launch**   **unusual**

3. Did you listen to the story on tape? If so, what kind of noises does Maxine hear and what does she see?

What happens when two ants leave their nest and do not return? Read about these two greedy characters.

Two Bad Ants

Two bad ants decide not to return to their nest after they travel with other ants to a kitchen to find sugar. They eat crystal after crystal until they fall asleep. When they wake, a spoon scoops them up and puts them into coffee. Before they get swallowed, the ants escape.

Then they climb inside a toaster. The ants think they will be cooked! But they pop out of the toaster and land on the faucet. They fall into the garbage disposal which suddenly goes on. But it stops quickly, and the ants climb out. The ants see something that reminds them of home. It's an electric socket. They climb in the holes and quickly get blown out. The two are too exhausted to go on.

The two ants hear their fellow ants returning. They quietly slip to the end of the line, get one crystal of sugar, and head for home, where they know they belong.

What Do You Think?

1. What words help you visualize where the ants are? Tell what would have happened if the ants hadn't escaped from the coffee. Share your story with a friend.

2. Retell the story using the words below. Draw a comic strip that retells an important scene from the story.

   crystal   **swallowed**   **escape**   **exhausted**

3. Did you listen to the story on tape? If so, did you ever think that the ants weren't going to escape?

Selection Summary Answer Key

How I Spent My Summer Vacation p. 40

1. Answers will vary, but students might say that Wallace made up the story because he had a wild imagination.

2. Answers will vary.

3. Possible answers: They cheered, shook his hand, and slapped his back.

Goldilocks and the Three Bears p. 41

1. Possible answers: Goldilocks was a bad girl. She did whatever she wanted without asking.

2. Answers will vary.

3. Possible answers: Papa Bear did not like it when he found out that somebody had been eating his porridge, sitting in his chair, and lying in his bed.

Anthony Reynoso: Born to Rope p. 42

1. Possible answers: Anthony rides and ropes. He can do rope tricks. He performs at shows. Anthony is like other kids because he goes to school. He collects basketball cards. He shoots baskets with his dad.

2. practice

3. Possible answers: Anthony visits his grandparents. He plays with his cousins. He has parties with his family.

Herbie and Annabelle p. 43

1. Annabelle keeps a sheet over her head so she can't see who her visitor really is.

2. pretended

3. Answers will vary. Students may say that they would be mad at Herbie because he wrote a story about a turkey and called the turkey Annabelle. Herbie gave Annabelle salmon for her birthday.

Allie's Basketball Dream p. 44

1. Possible answers: Allie is determined to make a basket. Students may say that Allie is a bad basketball player.

2. Answers will vary.

3. Possible answers: She cared about what they thought, but she didn't let it stop her.

Fly Traps! Plants That Bite Back p. 45

1. Possible answers: Some plants trap animals with trap doors, sticky leaves, leaves that snap close, and leaves that bugs can't climb out of.

2. Answers will vary.

3. Answers will vary, but students might say little yellow flowers, tangled stems with bubbles, bladderwort oozes, sticky like honey, spiky rim, cobras, fat red ones, thin yellow ones, curly green ones.

Selection Summary Answer Key

Guys from Space   p. 46

1. Answers will vary.

2. root beer

3. Possible answers: The space guys acted like real people when they drank root beer. The space guys also breathed air and spoke the kid's language.

Tornado Alert   p. 47

1. Answers will vary.

2 Answers will vary.

3. Possible answers: Stay away from metal pipes. If you are in school, follow directions.

Danger—Icebergs!   p. 48

1. Possible answers: An iceberg is hard to see because most of it is hidden. A ship could hit the iceberg.

2. Answers will vary.

3. Possible answers: The author described glaciers and ice packs, the loud boom of bubbles breaking in the holes of icebergs, the *Titanic* as it hit the iceberg, and where the iceberg traveled.

Nights of the Pufflings   p. 49

1. Possible answers: Halla and her friends do not see the chicks. The older birds feed the chicks fish. The chicks call for food. The pufflings try to fly to the sea and some get lost. Halla and her friends help rescue the pufflings.

2. rescue

3. Possible answers: They yell out the word *pufflings* in Icelandic. They use flashlights to find the pufflings in dark places. They run down the street to catch the birds. They take the birds home. Some pufflings nip at their fingers. They toss the birds up in the air for them to fly.

What Do Authors Do?   p. 50

1. Answers will vary.

2. Answers will vary.

3. Possible answers: They go to libraries, historical societies, and museums. They interview people.

Tops and Bottoms   p. 51

1. Answers will vary.

2. Answers will vary.

3. Possible answer: His father was wealthy and gave Bear his land and money.

Mom's Best Friend   p. 52

1. Possible answers: Ursula needs to form an attachment with Mom. Mom needs to train Ursula. Ursula needs to help Mom whenever she needs it.

2. guide

3. Possible answers: Yes, because she jumped on them and licked them.

Selection Summary Answer Key

Brave as a Mountain Lion   p. 53

1. Possible answers: Spider gets encouragement from his family. A spider tells him to listen to his spirit and not to be afraid.

2. brave

3. Possible answer: Spider went to the gym to see how scary it might be to be on stage during the spelling bee.

Your Dad Was Just Like You   p. 54

1. Answers will vary. Students might say that Peter finally understands his father because he fixes the trophy for him.

2. prove

3. Possible answers: He was having trouble in school. He didn't think he was smart, but he knew he was fast.

Ananse's Feast   p. 55

1. Answers will vary. Students might say yes, because Ananse and Akye invited each other over to eat. Students might say no, because they tricked each other.

2. Answers will vary.

3. Answers will vary. Students might say no, because they would float to the top of the water without eating. Students might say yes, because it is good manners to remove the robe.

Sam and the Lucky Money   p. 56

1. Winter. Sam and his mother are in Chinatown.

2. lucky

3. Answers will vary.

Thunder Cake   p. 57

1. The girl is afraid of the thunder. She decides that she was very brave while she gathered the ingredients for the cake.

2. Answers will vary.

3. Possible answers: Grandma reminds the girl that nothing will hurt her because she is there with her. She tells the girl not to pay attention to the thunder.

One Grain of Rice   p. 58

1. Possible answers: The raja breaks his promise to the people in the village. He takes their rice, but does not share it when they are hungry. The girl returns the rice to the people and saves them from hunger.

2. reward

3. Answers will vary. Students might say that the raja learned a lesson because he became wise and fair again.

Selection Summary Answer Key

The Woman Who Outshone the Sun   p. 59

1. Lucia was beautiful. She had black hair. She shone brighter than the sun. The river loved her. She was not mean. Answers to the second part of the question will vary.

2. thirst

3. Answers will vary. Students might say that they would help the people because the people were thirsty. The people were sorry about how they treated Lucia.

Flight: The Journey of Charles Lindbergh   p. 60

1. Answers will vary. Students might say they didn't think Lindbergh would make it because he may not have enough fuel, he almost fell asleep, he thought he was lost.

2. flight

3. Answers will vary.

Chibi: A True Story from Japan   p. 61

1. Possible answers: Chibi is the tiniest duck. She is afraid when the other ducks are not. She is everyone's favorite.

2. ducklings

3. Possible answers: Mr. Sato liked to take photographs. He knew that the mother duck planned to move her ducklings. He cared about the ducks because he stopped the traffic when the ducks crossed the street. He was disappointed when he didn't take a picture of the ducks crossing the street. He was happy that he was the one who helped the duck family.

Brave Irene   p. 62

1. A snowy place. The story would be different if it took place somewhere else because Irene wouldn't have had trouble delivering the dress.

2. Answers will vary.

3. Answers will vary.

Selection Summary Answer Key

More Than Anything Else   p. 63

1. Possible answers: Students might say that Booker will learn to read someday because he tells his mother he needs to learn to read. He studies the book his mother gives him and tries to figure out the sounds the black marks make. He looks for the newspaper man who can read and asks him about the alphabet.

2. alphabet

3. Answers will vary. Students might say that Booker works so hard that his arms hurt and he gets cuts from the salt.

Leah's Pony   p. 64

1. Answers will vary. Students might say it was a good idea for Leah to sell her pony because she helped save her family's farm. Students might say it was a bad idea because Leah would no longer have a pony.

2. Answers will vary.

3. Answers will vary. Students might say Leah could not buy a tractor for one dollar because they cost much more. She is able to buy the tractor because nobody bids against her.

The Piñata Maker   p. 65

1. No, you make the paste first.

2. Answers will vary.

3. Answers will vary.

Mailing May   p. 66

1. Answers will vary.

2. Answers will vary.

3. She tries to get a job at Alexander's Department Store.

The Extra-Good Sunday   p. 67

1. Answers will vary. Students might say Ramona and Beezus will not complain again because they learned that making a meal is hard.

2. Answers will vary.

3. Answers will vary.

Floating Home   p. 68

1. Answers will vary, but students might say that since Maxine traveled to space she did want to do well on her project.

2. Answers will vary.

3. Possible answers: Maxine heard rumbling, thunderous sounds, roars, loud booms, wind howling, and bangs. She saw everything on the ground getting smaller. She saw fire and smoke outside the windows, things floating in the cabin, and a shooting star.

Two Bad Ants   p. 69

1. Possible answers: spoon, coffee, toaster, faucet, garbage disposal, electric socket.

2. Answers will vary.

3. Answers will vary.

Before Reading

For an overview of the content and skills within the *Collection for Readers,* see pages 36–37 of this handbook.

Preview and Predict Turn to the title page of the selection. Read the title and question aloud. Then ask students to preview the illustrations. Model using the text, pictures, and question to predict what the story will be about. Then ask students to make their predictions.

Set Purposes Ask students to think about what they might like to learn about the characters or events illustrated in the pictures. Students can use the question on the title page, or write their own question, to set a purpose for reading.

Vocabulary Point out vocabulary words that might be important to understanding the story. (See lists on pp. 86–93 of this handbook.) Whenever possible, use the pictures to help students understand meanings of words. You may want to have students generate a list of words they don't know. Talk with students about the words to help them make connections between vocabulary and story concepts and what students already know. If you want to use additional vocabulary strategies with students, see page 13 of this handbook for ideas.

During Reading

Story Structure Remind students that fiction has a beginning, a middle, and an end. The story, or plot, centers on a problem, or conflict, that is resolved by the end of the story. Students can use story structure to make sense of, or understand, the story.

Characters Work with students to identify the main character(s). Have students look for clues about the characters based on what they say, what they do, and what others say about them. Encourage them to refer to pictures for clues.

Setting Help students look for information about the setting—where and when the story takes place. What words does the author use to reveal the setting? Help students find details in the pictures that correspond to the words. Ask students to think about how much time passes in the story.

Plot Tell students to look for the problem in the story. How is the problem solved? Encourage students to think about what is the most important part of the story.

Theme As students read, they should think "What is this story really about?"

© Scott Foresman 3

Summarize Information Help students synthesize information and make inferences about the text. You might ask:

- What are the important events in this part of the story?
- What is the author trying to tell you about the character(s)?
- What is this part of the story all about?
- What new things happened in this part of the story?

Locate and Classify Details Ask questions that prompt students to locate and classify details. Sample questions might be:

- What details can you find to support your thinking?
- Where in the story does it say that?
- What part of the story made you think that?

Critical Thinking Help students analyze the text. Ask questions like:

- Why do you think the author wrote this story?
- What is the problem in the story?
- How do the characters change?
- Is the problem resolved in a believable way?

Reread Have students reread the selection as necessary to build fluency and understanding.

Use the Take-Home Readers The Take-home version of the *Collection for Readers* can be used for rereading or activities such as coloring the pictures, and underlining key vocabulary.

After Reading

Discuss Talk with students about the predictions they made and the purpose they set for reading. Make connections to the topic or the unit theme of the selection.

Skill Practice Use Questions 1 and 2 in Looking Back to help students practice skills. See page 37 for an explanation of how Question 1 helps students routinely practice identifying the text or story structure and how Question 2 helps students practice five critical comprehension skills.

Critical Thinking Think About It or Talk About It, Question 3, asks students to think and talk critically about the story. Students relate the selection to their own lives or discuss their opinions about characters, plot, or theme with a partner. Sometimes students are asked to reflect about their own learning.

Before Reading

For an overview of the content and skills within the *Collection for Readers*, see pages 36–37 of this handbook.

Preview and Predict Read the story title aloud. Then ask students to preview the photographs, diagrams, and illustrations. Model using the text and pictures to predict what the selection will be about. Then ask students to make their predictions.

Set Purposes Ask students to think about what they already know about the topic. Remind students that what they already know about the topic will help them as they read. Then ask them what they would like to find out when they read the selection. You may want to have students use a K-W-L Chart or other graphic organizer. (See pp. 22–33 of this handbook.) Students can use the question on the title page, or write their own question, to set a purpose for reading.

Vocabulary Point out vocabulary words that might be important to understanding the selection. (See lists on pp. 86–93 of this handbook.) Whenever possible, use pictures and diagrams to help students understand meanings of words. You may want to have students generate a list of words they don't know. Talk with students about the words to help them make connections between vocabulary and selection concepts and what students already know about a topic. If you want to use additional vocabulary strategies with students, see page 13 of this handbook for suggestions.

During Reading

Text Structure Remind students that nonfiction selections provide information or explain something. Text structure refers to the way information is organized in a text. Students need to know how text is organized in order to find information. Show students how the author has organized information using titles, headings, captions, labels, questions, and other print features or graphic aids. Help students connect information in the text with photographs, diagrams, or illustrations.

Key Words Direct students to look for key words that signal the way the text is organized. Provide students with examples of key words to look for as they read.

Time Order: *first, next, before, after, last, later*

Cause and Effect: *because, since, as a result, due to, for this reason*

Compare and Contrast: *either, but, while, although, unlike*

Summarize Information Help students synthesize information and make inferences about the text. You might ask:

- What is the most important idea?
- What is the author trying to say?
- What is this part of the selection all about?
- What new things have you learned?

Locate and Classify Details Ask questions that prompt students to locate and classify details. Sample questions might be:

- What details can you find to support your thinking?
- Where in the selection does it say that?
- What are some of the important ideas?

Critical Thinking Help students analyze the text. Ask questions like:

- Why do you think the author wrote this selection?
- How is this like other selections you have read?
- What did the author do to make you interested in the topic?
- What questions do you still have about the topic?

Reread Have students reread the selection as necessary to build fluency and understanding.

See also **Use the Take-Home Readers,** page 77.

After Reading

Discuss Talk with students about the predictions they made and the purpose they set for reading. Make connections to the topic or the unit theme of the selection.

Skill Practice Use Questions 1 and 2 in Looking Back to help students practice skills. See page 37 for an explanation of how Question 1 helps students routinely practice identifying the text or story structure and how Question 2 helps students practice five critical comprehension skills.

Critical Thinking Think About It or Talk About It, Question 3, asks students to think and talk critically about the selection. This question leads students to think critically about the selection by relating it to their own lives or by discussing their opinions about people, events, or ideas with a partner. Some are metacognitive questions that help students reflect about their own learning.

Collection for Readers Answer Key

I Would Like to Visit a Fantastic Place

1. Possible answers: Characters—Alex, Mom; Problem—Alex can't decide where he wants to go for summer vacation when he finds a picture of a fantastic place; Events—Alex thinks he might like to go to the North Pole. But he thinks it might be too cold. He would like to go to Hawaii to swim with whales. But he thinks there might be sharks. He would like to go to a huge city. But he thinks there might be crowds. Alex's mom comes home; Solution—Alex finds out the picture is for his Aunt Pat. Alex's mom says they are going to the beach for the summer.

2. The North Pole; a huge city.

3. Answers will vary, but students should support their answers with details from the story or their own experience.

The City Mouse and the Country Mouse

1. Possible answers: Characters—City Mouse and Country Mouse; Settings—the country and the city; Events—City Mouse visits Country Mouse. City Mouse does not like Country Mouse's food, his bed, or going to the forest. He doesn't have fun. He invites Country Mouse to his big house in the city. At City Mouse's house, the two help themselves to a room full of food. A woman finds them and chases them into a hole; Ending—Country Mouse decides the city is not for him. He goes home. He is proud of his home and promises to stay there.

2. Possible answers: City Mouse's house is bigger than mine. It has a room filled with boxes of foods such as cookies, cereal, and popcorn. I usually eat berries and nuts. City Mouse has a quilt and pillow for a bed. I sleep on a bed of leaves.

3. Encourage students to look back in the story for details to support their ideas.

The Rodeo

1. Possible answers: Main idea—A rodeo is a great show where cowboys and cowgirls perform; Details—They do rope tricks, they ride wild horses, they try to win prizes.

2. Possible answers: Cowboys and cowgirls get to do rope tricks, ride bulls, rope calves, and win prizes. The people who watch can cheer for the cowboys and cowgirls.

3. Answers may vary, but students should support their answers with information from the article or their own experience.

Up All Night

1. Possible answers: Characters—Annie and Julia; Settings—inside Annie's house at night and outside the next morning; Events—Julia's mom lets her sleep over at Annie's house. Julia suggests that they stay up all night. Julia says they can play games all night. Annie says they can watch a video. The two make plans for the next day. They turn off the lights. They fall asleep; Ending—Annie and Julia wake up and go outside to watch the sun rise.

2. Possible answers: Annie and Julia wanted to do something special. They fell asleep.

3. Encourage students to look back in the story for details to support their ideas.

Girls Just Want to Play Hoops

1. Possible answers: Main idea—Sheryl Swoopes dreams of becoming a professional basketball player in the United States and finally does when the U.S. forms womens' basketball teams; Details—Sheryl dreamed of playing on a professional team in the United States.

© Scott Foresman 3

The U.S. didn't have professional women's teams, but finally forms teams in 1996. Sheryl joined the Houston Comets.

2. Possible answers: Sheryl played on the U.S. Olympic team. Sheryl knows how to shoot and move the ball on the court.

3. Encourage students to look back in the article for information to support their ideas.

Plant Traps!

1. Possible answers: Pitcher plant, Venus flytrap, sundew.

2. Possible answer: Some plants eat insects.

3. Students may say that the examples helped them to understand the main idea because they explained how plants eat insects.

ROCK from TOCK

1. Possible Answers: Characters—Eddie and ROCK; Settings—outside and Eddie's room; Events—Eddie wants someone to play with him. ROCK from the planet TOCK arrives. Eddie and ROCK play ball. ROCK cleans Eddie's room. ROCK helps Eddie use his computer to do homework. Eddie asks ROCK about planet TOCK. ROCK shows Eddie TOCK using the computer. ROCK gets a message from his dad saying it is time to go home; Ending— Eddie asks ROCK to come back soon because they were friends now.

2. Possible answers: Eddie and ROCK played ball, cleaned Eddie's room, and did homework on the computer.

3. Answers will vary.

Watch Out for Twisters!

1. Possible answers: Cause—Cool air meets warm air; Effect—A tornado may form; Cause—Tornadoes can spin up to 300 miles per hour; Effect—Tornadoes

can do great damage.

2. Possible answers: In the spring, the weather is changing from cool air into warm air. When cool air meets warm air, tornadoes can form.

3. Answers will vary.

Tip of the Iceberg

1. Possible answers: Main idea—Icebergs are pieces of ice in the ocean. Details— The tip of the iceberg only shows above water. Most of the iceberg is hidden beneath water. Ships can be damaged if they hit an iceberg.

2. Possible answer: The ship could hit the iceberg and be damaged.

3. Encourage students to look back in the article for details to include in their drawings.

Birds of the Water

1. Possible answers: Main idea—Some birds make the water their home; Details—Penguins, puffins, sea gulls, and flamingos live on or near water. Puffins only come to land once a year to lay eggs. Penguins spend most of their time swimming.

2. Possible answers: Penguins and flamingos live near water. Penguins use their wings to swim, flamingos do not.

3. Answers will vary, but students might say that the water is a good place for birds to swim, get food, and raise their babies. Students should support their answers with information from the article.

Making Pictures for a Book

1. Possible answers: Main idea— Illustrators draw the pictures that go into books; Details—Illustrators think about what the story is about before they draw. Illustrators decide what things should look like. Illustrators draw the pictures.

2. Possible answer: The illustrator wants to

© Scott Foresman 3

Collection for Readers Answer Key

make sure that the writer of the story likes the drawings.

3. Students may say that the book cover, title, pictures, and captions were clues that helped them know what the article would be about.

The Rabbit and the Turtle

1. Possible answers: Characters—rabbit, turtle, fox; Problem—The turtle is slower than the rabbit because he has shorter legs; Events—First, the turtle says he will race the rabbit. Next, the rabbit is far ahead of the turtle in the race. Then the rabbit thinks the turtle cannot catch up with him. He takes a rest and falls asleep. Last, the rabbit wakes up. The turtle is close to the finish. The rabbit cannot catch up; Solution—The turtle is slower, but he works harder than the rabbit to win the race.

2. Possible answers: The turtle is slow and the rabbit is fast. The turtle works hard and the rabbit doesn't.

3. Answers will vary, but students should support their answers with details from the story or their own experience.

Some Special Dogs

1. Possible answers: Main idea—Guide dogs are trained to help blind people; Details—Guide dogs go to Seeing Eye school to train. Guide dogs learn directions and how to cross streets. The owner and the dog learn to go places together.

2. Answers will vary, but students may say that a guide dog helps its owner cross the street and keeps its owner safe.

3. Encourage students to look back in the article for information to support their ideas.

Pretend You're Not Afraid

1. Possible answers: Characters—Kate, Mom, Dad, and Matt; Problem—Kate is afraid to give a school report; Events— First, Kate says she is afraid to give a speech. Next, Mom says she isn't afraid to give a speech because she looks at each person in the room. Then, Dad says he isn't afraid because he makes sure he has his facts right. Matt says he isn't afraid because he pretends he is not afraid. Last, Kate gives her speech and isn't afraid; Solution—Kate uses her family's ideas and isn't afraid when she makes her speech.

2. Possible answers: The people in Kate's class are her friends.

3. Answers will vary.

Good Game!

1. **This story is about:** Meg not trying hard enough when she played soccer; **This story takes place:** on the soccer field and in Meg's room. **The main events are:** It is rainy and cold during Meg's soccer game. Her team loses. Meg's Mom tells Meg she needed to try harder because her team needed her. Meg says she doesn't want to play soccer anymore. Meg tells her Gran that Mom is not happy with her. Gran says that Meg's mom used to play soccer and wants Meg to help her team; **The story ends when:** Meg tells her mom she should have tried harder.

2. Possible answers: Meg goes to her room. She talks to Gran about how her Mom used to play soccer.

3. Answers will vary.

Stone Soup

1. Possible answers: Characters—Alan, James, people from the town; a town; Events—Alan and James leave their home to find work. They find a stone. They get to a town where the people will not give them work or food. Alan comes up with an idea to get food. He makes

© Scott Foresman 3

82   Collection for Readers   Grade 3 • Answer Key

stone soup. A woman gives him a pot in exchange for some soup. People from the town gather to watch. The brothers invite them to a feast. They drop the stone in the pot. Two boys give them water. Another woman gives onions and carrots. A farmer gives meat and potatoes; Ending—everyone eats the soup.

2. Possible answer: The people in the town started sharing their food to make the soup. Then everyone ate until they were full.

3. Answers will vary.

Dragons for Breakfast

1. **This story is about:** how Scott tries to find the golden dragon in a box of cereal so he might win $100; **This story takes place:** at a grocery store and in Scott's kitchen; **The main events are:** Scott finds out about a contest from the back of a cereal box. He wants to find the golden dragon so he can win $100. Scott goes to the grocery store. He starts shaking all of the Red Dragon Delight cereal boxes. The store manager scolds him. Scott tells the manager what he is looking for. The manager lets Scott shake a few more boxes. Scott buys a box; **The story ends when:** Scott empties his cereal box, but doesn't find the golden dragon. Scott says he is lucky and may still find the golden dragon.

2. Possible answer: The manager is mad at first, but he is nicer when Scott tells him what he's looking for.

3. Encourage students to look back in the story for details to support their ideas.

Thunderstorms

1. Possible answers: Main idea—Weather changes during a thunderstorm; Details—Black clouds spread across the sky. Warm air bumps against cold air. Loud explosive noises happen.

2. Possible answers: The air around the lightning bolt gets hot; the arc moves quickly and spreads out, causing loud, explosive noises.

3. Answers will vary.

The Raja's Contest

1. **This story is about:** a raja who holds a thinking contest every year; **This story takes place:** in Punjab, a land in India; **The main events are:** the raja holds a thinking contest on his birthday. He makes a single line of rice using fifty grains. He says that the person who makes the line shorter without touching any grains will win a reward. Akbar thinks hard about the contest. Akabar discovers the answer. He goes to the palace. Akabar doubles the length of the raja's line by making a new line using one hundred grains of rice. The raja is pleased. Akabar is rewarded by the raja's daughter; **The story ends when:** Akbar falls in love with the raja's daughter and marries her.

2. Possible answers: The raja and Akbar both cannot sleep when they think about the contest.They both ask for tea and rice to eat. They both discover something about the contest from a bowl of rice. The raja is a king, Akbar is not. The raja is wealthy, Akbar is not.

3. Students may say that looking at the pictures first helps them understand what the story is about and gets them interested in reading it.

The Tale of Retaw Yob

1. Possible answers: Characters—Retaw Yob and Mike; Settings—town Fire Mountain; Events: Retaw Yob goes to the town where the fire is. He tells the people that he can put the fire out faster than anyone else. Big Mike says he can put the fire out faster. Retaw Yob says he can do it backwards. The two go up

© Scott Foresman 3

the mountain, carrying water. Retaw Yob walks backward. Big Mike walks forward. Retaw Yob is faster than Big Mike. The fire is put out by Retaw Yob; Ending—Two strangers tell Retaw about a fire in their town that they need help with.

2. Possible answer: Somebody probably told him about the fire.

3. Encourage students to look back in the story for details to support their ideas.

Charles Lindbergh—Making History

1. Possible answers: Main idea—Charles Lindbergh makes history by being the first person to fly solo from New York to Paris; Details—Nobody had every made the flight before. Lindbergh made the trip without stopping. He landed in Paris 33 1/2 hours after leaving New York.

2. Possible answer: If the plane were too heavy it would slow down and use more fuel, and Lindbergh might not make it to Paris.

3. Answers will vary.

Tokyo Today

1. Possible answers: Main idea—Tokyo is the biggest city in Japan and it's very crowded; Details—Tokyo is one of the largest cities in the world. Over 8 million people live in Tokyo. Cars, buses, and bicycles are everywhere.

2. Possible answers: The sidewalks are crowded. There's a lot of traffic. Tokyo doesn't have much room for houses.

3. Students may say that looking at the article first helps them understand what the article is about and gets them interested in reading it.

Snowdance

1. Event—Jamal meets Val outside in the snow; Event—They build a snowman and a snowlady. Event—Val has a dream that night about the snowman and snowlady coming to life and dancing with one another.

2. Possible answer: Val and Jamal decide to build more snowpeople. Students should use this event as the basis for the events that happen next.

3. Answers will vary, but students should support their answers with details from the story or their own experiences.

Booker T. Washington

1. Possible answers: Cause—Slavery ended; Effect—Booker's family left the plantation; Cause—Booker went to school and worked hard; Effect—He became a teacher.

2. Possible answer: Booker was a slave. Slaves were not allowed to go to school.

3. Answers will vary, but students should support their answers with information from the article or their own experience.

Hard Times on the Farm

1. Possible answers: Main idea—American farmers faced hard times in the 1920s and 1930s; Details—Prices for farm goods went down. Banks took their farms. A drought hit the plains.

2. Possible answers: Times were good in the 1900s because farmers could sell their crops and animals for good prices. Times were hard in the 1920s and 1930s because banks took farmers' land, farmers couldn't sell their crops and animals, and there was a drought.

3. Encourage students to look back in the article for information to support their answers.

Collection for Readers Answer Key

Fiesta Fun

1. Possible answers: Main idea—A fiesta is a party where people have a lot of fun; Details—There is music and dancing. People eat their favorite foods. Kids play a piñata game.

2. Possible answers: The piñata is filled with treats. After a child breaks the piñata with a stick, the children try to get the treats.

3. Answers will vary, but students should support their answers with information from the article or their own experience.

The Mail Must Go Through

1. Possible answers: Topic—mail delivery; Alike—Mail carriers deliver mail. People still get mail today; Different—Men on ponies used to transport mail. Now, people in trucks and planes do; Conclusion—How people get mail in the future will change.

2. Possible answer: Trains were faster than stagecoaches or the pony express.

3. Students may say that the graphic organizer helped them understand the different ways people delivered mail.

Brownies for Breakfast

1. **This story is about:** the Parker kids making breakfast for their Mom's birthday; **This story takes place:** at the Parker's house; **The main events are:** Ann, Mike, and Tim decide to make breakfast for their Mom's birthday. Tim insists on making brownies. Ann and Mike tell Tim that brownies are not for breakfast. Tim says the brownies would be Mom's birthday cake. Ann and Mike let him make the brownies. Mom is surprised by the breakfast and by the brownies; **The story ends when:** everyone eats brownies and agrees that Tim's brownies are a success.

2. Possible answers: Ann and Mike couldn't get Tim to help out with the breakfast, so they finally let him make brownies. Ann and Mike thought brownies would make a good birthday cake.

3. Answers will vary.

A View from Space

1. Possible answers: Main idea—Earth looks different from space; Details—Earth looks blue because of its many oceans. Astronauts can see lightning flash every minute. Earth looks like a big blue marble.

2. Possible answers: Earth looks green with lots of buildings and cars. Earth looks like a big blue marble from space.

3. Answers will vary, but students should support their answers with information from the story or their own experience.

Outside the Barn

1. **This story is about:** a cat named Charlie who likes to explore; **This story takes place:** inside and outside the barn; **The main events are:** Charlie's mother lets him explore outside. Charlie promises to stay in the neighborhood and not go to the garden, playground, or Skip's doghouse. He goes to the playground. He gets lost in the garden. He goes into Skip's doghouse; **The story ends when:** Charlie is chased back to the barn by Skip.

2. Possible answer: Charlie noticed Skip's doghouse and went inside. Skip chased Charlie back to the barn. Charlie ran inside the barn and up the steps to his mother. Charlie's mother scolded him.

3. Encourage students to look back in the story for details to support their ideas.

Unit 1 Selection 1

I Would Like to Visit a Fantastic Place

Comprehension Skill: Sequence

Vocabulary for Concept Development
summer
vacation
visit
crowds
fantastic
table

High-Frequency Words
would
though
like
picture
city
thought

Unit 1 Selection 2

The City Mouse and the Country Mouse

Comprehension Skill: Compare and Contrast

Vocabulary for Concept Development
breakfast
proud
country
city
forest

High-Frequency Words
have
with
and
the
big

Unit 1 Selection 3

The Rodeo

Comprehension Skill: Drawing Conclusions

Vocabulary for Concept Development
cowboy
cowgirl
horses
rodeo
rope
lariat
wild

High-Frequency Words
could
are
they
can
their
it

Unit 1 Selection 4

Up All Night

Comprehension Skill: Cause and Effect

Vocabulary for Concept Development
secret
special
friend
yawns
games
breakfast

High-Frequency Words
good
something
we
great
watch
play

Unit 1 Selection 5

Girls Just Want to Play Hoops

Comprehension Skill: Main ideas and Details

Vocabulary for Concept Development
professional
basketball
team
women
players

High-Frequency Words
many
there
her
with
but

Unit 2 Selection 1

Plant Traps!

Comprehension Skill: Main Idea and Details

Vocabulary for Concept Development
interesting
plant
soil
strange
minerals
insect

High-Frequency Words
what
need
grow
have
you

Unit 2 Selection 2

ROCK from TOCK

Comprehension Skill: Sequence

Vocabulary for Concept Development
neighborhood
scared
louder
flashlights
bored
someone

High-Frequency Words
can
help
clean
said
room
how

Unit 2 Selection 3

Watch Out for Twisters!

Comprehension Skill: Drawing Conclusions

Vocabulary for Concept Development
dangerous
storms
tornado
cloud
twister
forecasters
weather

High-Frequency Words
place
watch
this
down
people

Unit 2 Selection 4

Tip of the Iceberg

Comprehension Skill: Cause and Effect

Vocabulary for Concept Development
iceberg
glacier
float
Titanic
ocean
melt

High-Frequency Words
water
what
under
is
were
mean

Unit 2 Selection 5

Birds of the Water

Comprehension Skill: Compare and Contrast

Vocabulary for Concept Development
penguin
hatch
puffin
burrow
gulls
flamingo
chick

High-Frequency Words
are
do
water
to
young
their

Unit 3 Selection 1

Making Pictures for a Book

Comprehension Skill: Drawing Conclusions

Vocabulary for Concept Development
illustrator
colors
writer
paints
crayons
drawings

High-Frequency Words
picture
think
first
story
sometimes
they

Unit 3 Selection 2

The Rabbit and the Turtle

Comprehension Skill: Compare and Contrast

Vocabulary for Concept Development
shell
rabbit
turtle
steady
curve
race

High-Frequency Words
animals
around
knew
road
toward
warm

Unit 3 Selection 3

Some Special Dogs

Comprehension Skill: Main Idea and Details

Vocabulary for Concept Development
guide
harness
direction
attention
introduces
street

High-Frequency Words
together
school
some
help
make
happy

Unit 3 Selection 4

Pretend You're Not Afraid

Comprehension Skill: Cause and Effect

Vocabulary for Concept Development
lions
elephants
afraid
speech
pretend
report
facts

High-Frequency Words
something
about
give
sure
people
big

Unit 3 Selection 5

Good Game!

Comprehension Skill: Sequence

Vocabulary for Concept Development
soccer
field
cheered
bench
shivered
snack
rain

High-Frequency Words
don't
even
try
room
play
today

Unit 4 Selection 1

Stone Soup

Comprehension Skill: Sequence

Vocabulary for Concept Development
feast
share
brilliant
guests
stomach
boiling

High-Frequency Words
family
work
soon
their
said
were

Unit 4 Selection 2

Dragons for Breakfast

Comprehension Skill: Cause and Effect

Vocabulary for Concept Development
appreciate
dragon
lucky
manager
cereal
startled

High-Frequency Words
another
every
find
much
put

Unit 4 Selection 3

Thunderstorms

Comprehension Skill: Main Ideas and Details

Vocabulary for Concept Development
bolt
lightning
thunder
weather
miles

High-Frequency Words
hear
warm
across
sound
grow
very

Unit 4 Selection 4

The Raja's Contest

Comprehension Skill: Compare and Contrast

Vocabulary for Concept Development
bowl
double
grains
daughter
exclaimed
reward

High-Frequency Words
this
brought
every
sleep
thought

Unit 4 Selection 5

The Tale of Retaw Yob

Comprehension Skill: Drawing Conclusions

Vocabulary for Concept Development
arrived
astonished
forward
backwards
strange
respect

High-Frequency Words
carry
put
out
walked
was
water

© Scott Foresman 3

Unit 5 Selection 1

Charles Lindbergh, Making History

Comprehension Skill: Drawing Conclusions

Vocabulary for Concept Development
airplane
contest
engine
pilot
instruments
route

High-Frequency Words
between
had
off
ready
right
took

Unit 5 Selection 2

Tokyo Today

Comprehension Skill: Main Idea and Details

Vocabulary for Concept Development
commotion
office
pool
spring
traffic
emperor

High-Frequency Words
beautiful
city
make
much
always
very

Unit 5 Selection 3

Snowdance

Comprehension Skill: Sequence

Vocabulary for Concept Development
errand
strength
stumble
whirled
dream
trudging

High-Frequency Words
asked
finally
first
laughed
said

Unit 5 Selection 4

Booker T. Washington

Comprehension Skill: Cause and Effect

Vocabulary for Concept Development
alphabet
slavery
slave
plantation
newspapers
teacher
Civil War

High-Frequency Words
could
read
school
important
were
they

Unit 5 Selection 5

Hard Times on the Farm

Comprehension Skill: Compare and Contrast

Vocabulary for Concept Development
auction
borrowed
dust
soil
bid
plow

High-Frequency Words
children
many
people
work
they
down

Unit 6 Selection 1

Fiesta Fun

Comprehension Skill: Main Idea and Details

Vocabulary for Concept Development
fiesta
piñata
paste
covered
shaped
crepe paper

High-Frequency Words
paper
eat
our
people
many
they

Unit 6 Selection 2

The Mail Must Go Through

Comprehension Skill: Cause and Effect

Vocabulary for Concept Development
train
station
mailbag
bundled
mail carrier
carted

High-Frequency Words
was
place
has
took
from

Unit 6 Selection 3

Brownies for Breakfast

Comprehension Skill: Drawing Conclusions

Vocabulary for Concept Development
refrigerator
breakfast
kitchen
brownies
success

High-Frequency Words
little
something
want
make
put

© Scott Foresman 3

Unit 6 Selection 4

A View from Space

Comprehension Skill: Compare and Contrast

Vocabulary for Concept Development
rocket
shuttle
astronaut
weigh
launch
fuel

High-Frequency Words
because
different
have
important
work

Unit 6 Selection 5

Outside the Barn

Comprehension Skill: Sequence

Vocabulary for Concept Development
sparkling
dangerous
explore
neighborhood
playground
corner

High-Frequency Words
morning
mother
found
enough
saw

Collection for Readers
Grades 3-6

Comprehension Skill	Grade 3	Grade 4	Grade 5	Grade 6
Cause and Effect	*Unit 1* Up All Night *Unit 2* Tip of the Iceberg *Unit 3* Pretend You're Not Afraid *Unit 4* Dragons for Breakfast *Unit 5* Booker T. Washington *Unit 6* The Mail Must Go Through	*Unit 1* Snow on the Prairie *Unit 2* Life on the Prairie *Unit 3* A Dangerous Storm *Unit 4* How Earth Learned to Sing *Unit 5* American Peddlers *Unit 6* A Rockin' Good Time	*Unit 1* The Negro Leagues *Unit 2* Hurricane! *Unit 3* The First Day *Unit 4* Pizza with Grandma *Unit 5* A Famous Messenger *Unit 6* The Garden Wall	*Unit 1* The Potter's Hands *Unit 2* Thirsty Land *Unit 3* Super Women of Sports *Unit 4* We Are All One *Unit 5* The Real Cowboy *Unit 6* Making a Light in the Darkness
Compare and Contrast	*Unit 1* The City Mouse and the Country Mouse *Unit 2* Birds of the Water *Unit 3* The Rabbit and the Turtle *Unit 4* The Raja's Contest *Unit 5* Hard Times on the Farm *Unit 6* A View from Space	*Unit 1* Just Like Home *Unit 2* City Gardens *Unit 3* The Greatest Lumberjack Ever *Unit 4* The Three Little Pigs and the Big Bad Wolf *Unit 5* Early Cars *Unit 6* American Inventions	*Unit 1* My Friend Marissa *Unit 2* Playful Pals *Unit 3* The Cat That Was Part Dog *Unit 4* Dinner with the Tanakas *Unit 5* The Fight to Vote *Unit 6* Break a Leg!	*Unit 1* Starting Over *Unit 2* Survival Skills *Unit 3* The Lot *Unit 4* The Lady with the Lamp *Unit 5* A Trip to Remember *Unit 6* Demetrius of Alexandria
Drawing Conclusions	*Unit 1* The Rodeo *Unit 2* Watch Out for Twisters *Unit 3* Making Pictures for a Book *Unit 4* The Tale of Retaw Yob *Unit 5* Charles Lindbergh, Making History *Unit 6* Brownies for Breakfast	*Unit 1* Come to a Fiesta! *Unit 2* A Friendly, Furry Pet *Unit 3* Tiger in the Moonlight *Unit 4* Korea Today *Unit 5* North to the Pole *Unit 6* The Boy Who Dreamed	*Unit 1* Little Italy *Unit 2* Wetlands *Unit 3* The Iron Horse *Unit 4* Born to Run *Unit 5* Sugihara's Visas *Unit 6* Real Art	*Unit 1* Japanese Americans *Unit 2* Oil Spills: Slick and Deadly *Unit 3* The Story of Elizabeth Blackwell *Unit 4* Something from Nothing *Unit 5* Mars and Martians *Unit 6* When Grandma Came to Stay

© Scott Foresman 3

Comprehension Skill	Grade 3	Grade 4	Grade 5	Grade 6
Main Idea and Details	*Unit 1* Girls Just Want to Play Hoops *Unit 2* Plant Traps! *Unit 3* Some Special Dogs *Unit 4* Thunderstorms *Unit 5* Tokyo Today *Unit 6* Fiesta Fun	*Unit 1* New Homes for Orphans *Unit 2* Monsters, Dragons, and Other Reptiles *Unit 3* Heroes of the Pampas *Unit 4* Lucky Lou *Unit 5* Where Are We? *Unit 6* Native American Art	*Unit 1* The First Orphan Train *Unit 2* Make the World a Better Place *Unit 3* Making Honey *Unit 4* Run Like the Wind *Unit 5* A Woman Named Harriet *Unit 6* Are You going to Eat That?	*Unit 1* The Right Man for the Job *Unit 2* Save the Sea Turtle *Unit 3* Planets in a Row *Unit 4* The Wonder of Ancient Egypt *Unit 5* Life at the Pole *Unit 6* From Blueprints to Buildings
Sequence	*Unit 1* I Would Like to Visit a Fantastic Place *Unit 2* ROCK from TOCK *Unit 3* Good Game! *Unit 4* Stone Soup *Unit 5* Snowdance *Unit 6* Outside the Barn	*Unit 1* Chores Can Be Fun *Unit 2* City Cousin and Country Cousin *Unit 3* Timber! *Unit 4* I Was There *Unit 5* Sea Turtles *Unit 6* Gone from the Patio	*Unit 1* A Great Invention *Unit 2* The Ripe Red Apple Mystery *Unit 3* You Go, Girl! *Unit 4* The Sunrise Dance *Unit 5* A Trip to the Museum *Unit 6* The Weak Old Woman	*Unit 1* Cassey at Camp *Unit 2* Something to Crow About *Unit 3* Last Man Up in Mudville *Unit 4* Why the Wildflowers Grow *Unit 5* Nightmare on Dessert Island *Unit 6* The Aliens

© Scott Foresman 3

Leveled Readers 1–6

Comprehension Skill	Leveled Readers for Grade 1	Leveled Readers for Grade 2	Leveled Readers for Grade 3	Leveled Readers for Grade 4	Leveled Readers for Grade 5	Leveled Readers for Grade 6
Author's Purpose	5A, 5B, 16A, 16B	33A, 33B	63A, 63B, 84A, 84B	94A, 94B, 114A, 114B, 120A, 120B	124A, 124B, 140A, 140B	170A, 170B
Cause and Effect	2A, 2B, 6A, 6B, 22A, 22B, 24A, 24B	43A, 43B	64A, 64B, 78A, 78B	97A, 97B	124A, 124B	153A, 153B, 163A, 163B
Character	12A, 12B	32A, 32B, 44A, 44B, 52A, 52B	65A, 65B	95A, 95B	122A, 122B, 131A, 131B	155A, 155B, 175A, 175B
Compare and Contrast	7A, 7B, 20A, 20B, 27A, 27B	36A, 36B, 38A, 38B	79A, 79B	93A, 93B, 107A, 107B	136A, 136B	162A, 162B
Context Clues	1A, 1B, 11A, 11B	42A, 42B, 57A, 57B	68A, 68B	100A, 100B	139A, 139B, 144A, 144B	172A, 172B
Drawing Conclusions	8A, 8B 30A, 30B	35A, 35B	62A, 62B	102A, 102B, 105A, 105B	130A, 130B	161A, 161B
Fact and Opinion		53A, 53B	69A, 69B, 82A, 82B	118A, 118B	128A, 128B	171A, 171B, 180A, 180B
Generalizing			75A, 75B	103A, 103B	123A, 123B	154A, 154B, 176A, 176B
Graphic Sources		39A, 39B, 54A, 54B	66A, 66B	113A, 113B	127A, 127B, 132A, 132B	178A, 178B
Main Idea and Supporting Details	9A, 9B, 15A, 15B, 23A, 23B	51A, 51B, 55A, 55B	70A, 70B	119A, 119B	137A, 137B	168A, 168B
Making Judgments		50A, 50B, 60A, 60B	81A, 81B	101A, 101B	149A, 149B	156A, 156B
Paraphrasing				106A, 106B	142A, 142B, 145A, 145B	179A, 179B
Plot	17A, 17B, 28A, 28B	49A, 49B, 58A, 58B	85A, 85B, 89A, 89B	110A, 110B, 112A, 112B	133A, 133B, 148A, 148B	167A, 167B
Predicting	3A, 3B, 19A, 19B	31A, 31B	80A, 80B, 83A, 83B	104A, 104B	138A, 138B	157A, 157B
Sequence	21A, 21B, 25A, 25B	40A, 40B	61A, 61B	92A, 92B	121A, 121B	151A, 151B
Setting	4A, 4B	34A, 34B	77A, 77B, 87A, 87B	91A, 91B	141A, 141B	158A, 158B
Steps in a Process		37A, 37B	71A, 71B, 86A, 86B	117A, 117B	126A, 126B, 147A, 147B	173A, 173B
Summarizing		41A, 41B, 45A, 45B	72A, 72B	109A, 109B, 111A, 111B	135A, 135B	164A, 164B, 174A, 174B
Text Structure			73A, 73B	98A, 98B, 108A, 108B, 115A, 115B	134A, 134B	169A, 169B
Theme	14A, 14B, 26A, 26B, 29A, 29B	47A, 47B, 59A, 59B	76A, 76B	99A, 99B	146A, 146B	165A, 165B
Visualizing			74A, 74B, 88A, 88B	96A, 96B, 116A, 116B	143A, 143B, 150A, 150B	159A, 159B

Each of the above Leveled Readers has its own instructional plan in the Leveled Reader Resource Guide.

© Scott Foresman 3